CARD GAMES
for kids

hamlyn

CARD GAMES
for kids

Adam Ward

In memory of Adam Ward, 1970–2004

First published in Great Britain in 2004 by
Hamlyn, an imprint of Octopus Publishing Group Ltd
2–4 Heron Quays, London E14 4JP

Distributed in the United States and Canada by
Sterling Publishing Co., Inc.
387 Park Avenue South, New York, NY 10016–8810

ISBN 0 600 61074 8
EAN 9780600610748

A CIP catalogue record for this book is available from the
British Library

WADDINGTONS NO. 1 PLAYING CARDS ©
2004 Hasbro International Inc.
Used with kind permission of Hasbro.

COOP BOLD and COOP BLACK fonts © and ™
2004 House Industries

Printed and bound in Dubai

10 9 8 7 6 5 4 3 2 1

CONTENTS

INTRODUCTION

Entertaining kids is not an easy task. The unrelenting combination of unsappable energy, inexhaustible inquisitiveness and goldfish-like concentration can make us believe there is no other choice but to sit our youngsters down (preferably with siblings in separate rooms) and let a shiny Disney DVD take charge. We've all done it ...

'OK,' you're thinking, 'so this is where you tell us that 52 playing cards are the answer to our parenting prayers?' No, not exactly. But you may be surprised at how absorbed even the most demanding youngsters can become while playing a well-chosen and clearly explained game.

Timing is the key to success. Introducing a new game to tired children or those charged with tartrazine and sugar will lead only to chaos and frustration. Choose your time carefully, clear the playing area and make sure that you are fully conversant with the rules yourself. Ideally, you should always play every game before you start teaching your children.

Selecting the right game is also vital. You must find a game that is challenging but which they can understand and play without too much preamble and prevarication. Whenever possible, try to get them playing with simplified rules before adding in greater refinement as they get used to the gameplay. For example, you can start by introducing them to simple trick-playing games with a hand of trumps, then add in stakes and finally move them onto simple variants of Whist (see page 48). This kind of progression should help ensure a steady learning curve and a similarly satisfying tempo to the play. Now all you've got to do is convince them that it is time to put down the remote and take up a fresh challenge.

EDUCATIONAL VALUE

Claims about 'learning through play' always sound a bit trite; like the words of overpaid, under-informed marketing types who use phrases such as 'added value' and 'desired learning outcomes' to make you buy a brightly coloured plastic toy dinosaur that speaks with a computer-generated American West-coast accent.

But when it comes to card games, your children really will boost their brainpower. If a child wants to win (and believe me, non-competitive youngsters are as rare as snow in the Sahara), card games will invariably provide a rigorous test of both memory and arithmetic. Some games, like Rummy (see page 62), will test both qualities equally, while others like Pontoon (see page 102) or 31s (see page 98) provide a more obvious demand for mathematical ability. Either way, your children really will be learning as they play ... totting up their cards, working on sequences and trying to recall which cards have been played and which are still sought.

Whisper it ... but it all sounds like a marketing man's fantasy ... a compact, lightweight gaming system which is inexpensive and durable and that provides entertainment with simultaneous educational benefits. Did I mention the 'desired learning outcomes that provide added value'?

THE WHY QUESTION

Younger children will inevitably start any card game with a series of why questions: 'Why is the Ace worth one and 11?'; 'Why has that one got a sword?'; 'What are clubs and spades?'; 'Why are there jokers and why don't we ever seem to use them?' You will never be able to answer all their quirky questioning, but if you have some well-chosen facts and a little bit of background trivia, you may be able to bluff it sufficiently well to retain their interest. So, without further ado, here's some background knowledge to keep you one step ahead of your interrogators.

A LITTLE HISTORY

The earliest evidence of card playing has been found in China, with Central Asia soon following suit (if you'll pardon the pun). The first cards were simple paper dominoes found in China. Europe got its first taste of the new craze in the 14th century when Islamic-influenced packs, complete with court cards, appeared in Italy and Spain. We know that card games arrived in Europe at around this time because soon afterwards several courts in Italy and Switzerland outlawed the playing of such heretical games.

US INFLUENCE

According to many experts, card players have the United States to thank for refining playing cards. Americans are apparently responsible for rounding the corners of our cards and adding varnish to make them more durable. The US influence is also reputed to be responsible for making the court cards double-headed and inventing jokers (though this claim is not without some dissent).

SUITS

The four suits (spades, clubs, diamonds and hearts) that are commonly found in British cards are said to have their origins in France.

There are many theories about what each of the various suits represents. One fairly persuasive theory says that each corresponds to one of the four classes of medieval society. The spades, which represent swords or spearheads (weapons of knights), are the aristocracy; hearts stand for the church; diamonds are a sign of the wealthy (apparently the rich had diamond-shaped paving stones above their graves); and clubs, which are said to signify clover (the food of pigs), represent the peasantry.

VARIATONS ON THE SUITS

Spades, clubs, diamonds and hearts may be the norm in England and France, but elsewhere in Europe the four suits often vary, with the following more common national variations:

GERMANY – hearts, leaves, bells, acorns
SWITZERLAND – shields, flowers, bells, acorns
SPAIN/ITALY – swords, batons/clubs, cups, coins

TAROT

Tarot cards and playing cards are closely linked. The practice of reading tarot cards in layout style for the purposes of fortune-telling first arose at the same time that patience games of the same ilk appeared.

ROYAL MODELS

The four Kings have also been said to represent various historical characters. The most popular theory is that the four Kings depicted on the common French-influenced cards are: Charlemagne (hearts), David (spades), Caesar (diamonds) and Alexander (clubs). The

Queens are thought to be Judith (hearts), Pallas (spades), Rachel (diamonds) and Argine (clubs). The Knaves (Jacks) are La Hire (hearts), Ogier (spades), Hector (diamonds) and Lancelot (clubs).

DEADMAN'S HAND

A hand of cards made up of black Aces and eights is popularly known as a 'deadman's hand'. The reason for this somewhat morbid moniker is that it was the collection of cards held by notorious Western gunman Wild Bill Hickock when he was shot dead during a Poker game in a saloon in August 1876. Whenever a card player holds such a hand, he or she is likely to feel a little uneasy … and will usually be compelled to take a glance over his or her shoulder.

ETIQUETTE

Card games, like most games, depend on rules and on certain protocols to ensure that they run smoothly and without impropriety. Children do not need to be overly burdened with the minutiae of card game etiquette, but they should understand the basics.

SHUFFLING

There are many ways to shuffle cards, some complicated, some simple, but the most commonly employed and efficient is the rifle shuffle. Split the cards into two roughly equal piles, placing one in your left hand and one in your right. The backs of the cards are placed on a table and the thumbs rifle through the front edge of the cards, interleaving the two stacks together. The interleaved cards are pushed together to make a neat pile of 52 shuffled cards. According to mathematicians, you need to shuffle a deck of cards seven times to completely randomize them.

CUTTING

The practice of cutting cards prior to dealing is straightforward and should be comprehensible to any child over the age of four. One player simply takes a pile of cards (it must be more than four cards but less than 48) from the top of the deck and places it under the remainder of the cards. Simple. Players should cut the deck before and after shuffling and also to determine the dealer.

DEALING

The most usual way to determine who deals a particular hand is for each player to cut the deck and reveal the bottom card from the stack of cards lifted. The player who shows the lowest card gets the job (though the convention for some games is for the player with the highest card to become dealer). If two players draw cards of identical rank, they both cut again and continue doing so until one has a lower card.

The job of dealer should rotate round the table in a clockwise direction, with the player to the left of the first dealer taking charge for the second hand.

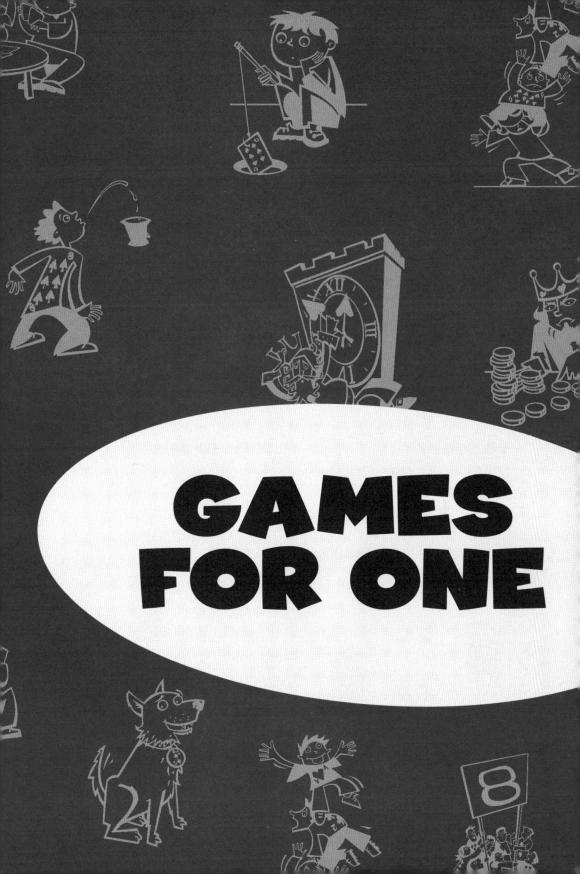

GAMES FOR ONE

 KLONDIKE

OR CANFIELD, PATIENCE, SOLITAIRE

AGES: 10+

SKILL LEVEL:

GOOD FOR: Rainy days and train journeys.

This is probably the best-known and most popular patience game. It's very hard to win, and will be a real test.

AIM OF THE GAME:

To get all the cards from your hand and the layout into four piles, one for each suit, with the Ace on the bottom and King on top.

TO START

1. Shuffle the pack and deal out 28 cards, as below:

HOW TO PLAY

1. If you see any Aces face up, put them above your layout (to start your four foundation piles). Then turn over any cards

FOUNDATION PILES

STOCK

When you have dealt, place the rest of the pack in front of you – this is called your stock.

underneath the Aces you took out. If there are any twos now, put those onto the aces of the same suit.

2. Next, put any cards that are one less in number directly underneath the higher cards (eights under nines, fives under sixes etc). **BUT NOTE!** They have to be opposite colours (so red must have black under it, and black has to have a red under it).

3. When you've done all you can, deal three cards from your stock face down and turn the pile up. If the top card of your new pile can go onto your layout, play it. The second card then comes into play. If you can't play the top card, deal three new cards.

The good thing is you can move whole columns of cards within the layout, or parts of columns, so you can get to a card you want to play.

4. Kings can be put on the blank spaces left if you've moved a whole column onto a foundation pile.

WHEN HAVE YOU WON?

When all the cards have been put onto the four foundation piles, topped with the King of their suit. Then gather up the cards, shuffle them really well (because remember they're all in number order!) and deal a fresh layout.

WE DID SAY IT WAS TOUGH!

TOP CHEATING TIPS

Naughty? Yes. But remember you'll only be cheating yourself! When you've found you can't move the cards around any more, go through the stock one card at a time rather than three; or if you really have reached your wit's end, look through the face-down piles, find a two, and play it.

DUNDEE
OR SECOND GUESS

AGES: 5+

SKILL LEVEL: ▮▮

GOOD FOR: Whiling away time on trains, planes and automobiles.

Dundee is a compelling game of chance which will keep kids occupied for hours, and what's more, it's simple and can be played almost anywhere.

AIM OF THE GAME:
To turn over all 52 cards in a pack without predicting one correctly ... sounds a bit bizarre, but trust me, it will make sense!

TO START

1. Shuffle the cards and settle down ... you will be playing for some time.

HOW TO PLAY

1. Hold the shuffled deck face down.

2. Before turning over the first card, you must announce a rank of card, for example, 'Five'. Say the word out loud and be clear – you will only cheat yourself if you mumble or kid yourself that you've forgotten what you said.

3. You must try to avoid predicting the card you are about to turn over. If your announcement coincides with the rank of card revealed, your turn reaches an immediate end. So, back to our example, if you'd announced 'Four' and then turned over the four of hearts, the game's up. The then cards must be shuffled again and the game recommences.

4. The game continues in this way until either you predict a card or you get through the entire deck. This latter situation is extremely rare. The game is also made harder by the rule that you cannot make the same prediction in consecutive turns.

WHEN HAVE YOU WON?

When you've turned over the entire deck and have no cards held in hand. If you don't make it to the end of the pack, you can count up the remaining cards and make a mental note of how close you got. Keep trying to beat your personal best and, if you've got a sibling to play against, see if you can outperform them.

ACES UP
OR IDIOT'S DELIGHT

AGES: 7+

SKILL LEVEL: ▓▓▓

GOOD FOR: Patience players with small tables.

A simple patience game that is quick to set up and can be played almost anywhere.

AIM OF THE GAME:
To discard cards from the layout until you have only the Aces left.

TO START

1. Deal four cards face up onto a table from a shuffled deck. The four face-up cards are your layout in Aces Up.

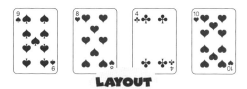

LAYOUT

2. Hold the remaining cards face down in your hand.

CHEAT YOURSELF

If the game becomes blocked, younger players should be given one free move; in other words they are allowed to discard the lowest-ranked card in the layout irrespective of suit. If this doesn't get the game moving again, it's time to gather up the cards, shuffle and re-deal.

HOW TO PLAY

1. If any of the four cards in the layout are from the same suit, you can discard all but the highest ranked of them (Aces are high). So, for example, if the four cards were the King of hearts, the Jack of clubs, the four of hearts and the two of clubs, you would discard the latter two cards.

2. Gaps in the layout are filled with cards from the stack.

3. The game continues in this way, with cards, discarded and replaced until either the cards are exhausted or the game becomes blocked.

WHEN HAVE YOU WON?

A successful game ends when the layout is made up of the four Aces.

STOP THE CLOCK
OR THE CLOCK, CLOCK PATIENCE

AGES: 7+

SKILL LEVEL: ▌▌▌

GOOD FOR: A little suspense on a rainy day.

Straightforward rules and a swift outcome make this an addictive solo game for younger players.

AIM OF THE GAME:
To turn over all the cards on the clockface before you uncover the fourth King.

TO START

1. Shuffle the pack and deal out the cards into 13 piles of four cards each. Twelve of the piles should be set out face down in a circle that approximates a clockface. The remaining set of four cards is then placed in the middle of the layout.

HOW TO PLAY

1. Start the game by turning over the top card in the central pile. Suppose the card turned over is a six, you must then place that card face up under the pile of cards at the bottom of the clockface layout (in the position that corresponds to six o'clock on a conventional dial).

2. Having laid down your six, you continue the game by turning over the top card of the same pile. The revealed card is placed under the relevant pile and the top card turned over and relocated to its home.

3. When you reveal the fourth card in a pile and there is no face-down card left to turn over, you turn over the top card of the next highest pile in the layout.

WHEN HAVE YOU WON?

You win the game if you manage to get all 12 piles of cards on the circular layout face-up. You lose the game if you turn over the fourth King before you have managed to get the circular layout complete. Simple really – it's you against the Kings.

FINISHED PILES

UNFINISHED PILES

TAKING YOUR TIME

There's nothing more annoying than getting halfway through a game only to find that you'd earlier put a card in the wrong position. Once you've made a mistake the game cannot be continued, so take your time and do not rush. Younger players may benefit from having a watch or clockface to refer to when playing; alternatively, you might like to draw out the layout on a piece of paper so that they have a model to follow. It is also imperative that the cards are spaced evenly, without overlapping, and that the game is played on a flat surface.

GOLF

AGES: 8+

SKILL LEVEL: ▮▮▮

GOOD FOR: Competitive types who enjoy a sporting challenge.

Easy to set up, addictive and with the option of a head-to-head two-player version, Golf with cards is more fun than hitting a small ball around a park in the cold.

AIM OF THE GAME:
To remove as many cards as possible from the layout before the cards in hand run out.

TO START

1. Shuffle the pack and deal out seven rows of five cards overlapping and face up. This 35-card layout is called the links. The remainder of the cards are held in hand (face down) and dealt one by one onto a waste pile. The objective of the game is to move the cards in the links onto the waste pile.

HOW TO PLAY

1. Turn over the first card held in hand. The card revealed is used to start the waste pile and this can be built on with any of the exposed cards (the bottom card in each column) in the links.

2. Place the cards moved from the links face up on top of the waste pile. You can play cards out of the layout in either ascending or descending order and irrespective of suit. So, for example, if the card on top of the waste pile is a four of diamonds, you could add either a five or three of any suit to it from the links.

3. When a card has been removed from the bottom row of the links, the card beneath it becomes available for play.

4. Continue adding to the pile by moving cards from the links until there are no cards left that you can play. The sequence can go up and down at will, so just because the first card added to that four of diamonds was a five, you don't have to keep going up. A five can be followed by a four and then another five, and so on.

5. Aces are low (that is, they count as one), and they can only be added to by a two;

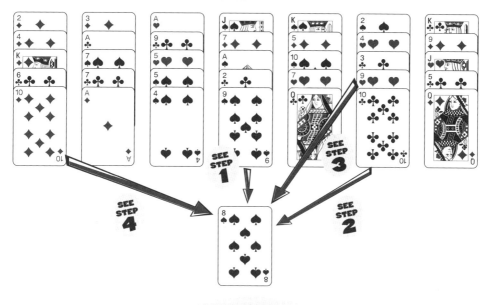

WASTE PILE

Kings, similarly, can only be built on by a Queen. In other words, you can't take the sequence 'round the corner' (King-Ace-two).

6. When you've exhausted all the available moves, turn over the next card held in hand and add it to the waste pile.

7. Continue playing until either the links are empty or your stock of cards in hand has run out.

SCORING

You calculate your score for the hole (hand) by counting up the cards left in the links at the end of play. If, however, you manage to empty the layout, you count up the cards left in hand and award yourself a minus score. Just as in real golf, low scores are best. Ideally, you should aim to play 18 holes for a complete round. Keep a note of your score and see if you can get a score of less than 72 strokes for the round.

TWO-PLAYER OPTION

The great thing about Golf patience is that it can also be played competitively as a two-player game. You'll need two packs of cards, a large table and a couple of hours, but the rewards are worthwhile.

1. Each player deals out his or her cards as above and the two hands are played simultaneously.

2. You can either record the scores for each hole, and the player with the lowest aggregate score at the end of '18 holes' is the winner, or you can adopt 'matchplay' scoring.

3. Under matchplay rules, each hole is either won, lost or halved (drawn), so at any stage a player is 'two up', 'four down' or a similar score as in the real matchplay game. The round continues until one player has an unassailable lead.

PUSS IN THE CORNER

AGES: 8+

SKILL LEVEL: ▋▋▋

GOOD FOR: Players who want a patience game that is both winnable and demanding.

A solo card game that is challenging without being impossible is a rare gem indeed ... Puss In The Corner is just such a game.

AIM OF THE GAME:

To build onto the four Aces in sequence and colour (though not suit) until all 52 cards are in the layout.

TO START

1. Separate out the four Aces from a standard deck of cards and place them in a square in the centre of a large, clear table. The Aces are the foundation cards in this game and are built upon in ascending order.

2. The remaining 48 cards are shuffled and placed face down in the player's hand.

HOW TO PLAY

1. Turn over the cards held in hand one by one. Cards can be played onto the layout if they follow in sequence and are matched in colour, so, for example, a two of hearts can be played onto either the Ace of hearts or the Ace of diamonds.

2. If the card revealed cannot be added to the layout, it is placed face up into one of four waste piles positioned at the corners of the four Aces (see diagram opposite).

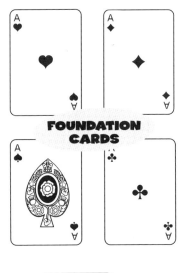

FOUNDATION CARDS

HAND

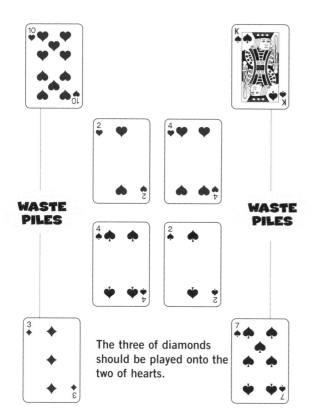

WASTE PILES

WASTE PILES

The three of diamonds should be played onto the two of hearts.

WINNING WAY

The key to success in this game is to make sure you organize your waste piles properly. Group the cards as outlined below to start with, but as the game develops you will need to think more tactically. If you empty a waste pile, for example, you may want to fill the space with a card that you will soon be needing. Similarly, you may want to avoid covering a card that will soon become playable. Think ahead and try to keep your options open.

3. When the opportunity arises, the top card from any of the waste piles can be played onto the layout.

4. Players should try to play cards of similar rank onto particular waste piles. One pile should be reserved for cards ranked two to four; the next for cards five to seven; the next for cards ranked eight, nine and ten; and the last for court cards. By adopting this approach, players reduce the likelihood of finding themselves blocked later in the game.

5. Play continues in this fashion until the stock of cards runs out. The cards are then gathered up from the four waste piles (take care to place the lowest-rank pile at the top of the stack). Cards from the new stack are turned over one by one and are either played onto the layout or a single waste pile. The top card from the waste pile can be played onto the layout at any time.

6. If you have grouped your cards sensibly, it should be possible to get the remainder of the cards into the layout without too much effort. But you only get one deal, so when the stack of cards has been emptied onto the layout and the waste pile, that's your lot.

WHEN HAVE YOU WON?

When all 52 cards in the deck have made it onto the layout, the game is complete. You should win more games than not. If you can't bear losing, however, you can always give yourself one more chance to go through the waste pile.

BISLEY

AGES: 10+

SKILL LEVEL: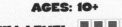

GOOD FOR: Bright kids who need a break from computers and other techno gadgets.

Bisley is a patience classic which will test the brainpower of adults and children alike.

AIM OF THE GAME:

To move all the cards from the layout onto foundation cards of Aces and Kings. Players build from the Aces in ascending order and from the Kings in descending order. Cards must be built in suit.

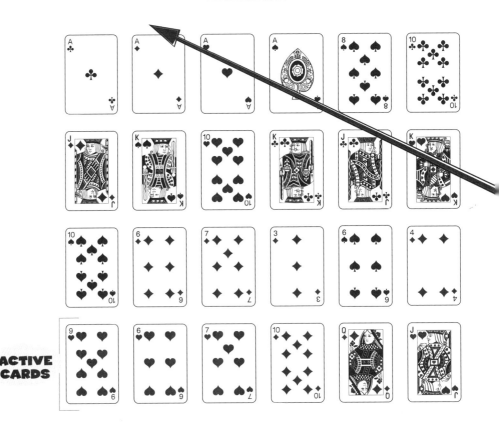

ACTIVE CARDS

TO START

1. Remove the Aces from the pack and lay them out (in any order) as the first four cards in a row of 13. Lay the cards face up and add three further rows of 13, with cards forming columns of four cards each.

HOW TO PLAY

1. The bottom card in each column is active and can be moved either onto the foundation piles (the Aces at the top of the layout) or can be used to build on other columns. Players can build on columns either up or down, but the card moved must be of the same suit as the one it joins (unlike games like Klondike, page 12, which build in alternating colours).

2. The player's first objective should be to free the Kings from the layout. When a King is exposed, it is moved to the top of the

board and positioned directly above the corresponding Ace. The King becomes a second foundation card and can be built on in descending order.

3. Only single cards can be moved. Shifting whole or part of a column is not allowed.

4. The space left vacant by the removal of the last card in a column is not filled.

WHEN HAVE YOU WON?

Success arrives when you have removed all the cards from the layout onto the foundation piles. It doesn't matter whether you build more cards onto the Ace or the King of a particular suit and it is irrelevant where the two sequences meet. If there are no cards left in the layout, you've won.

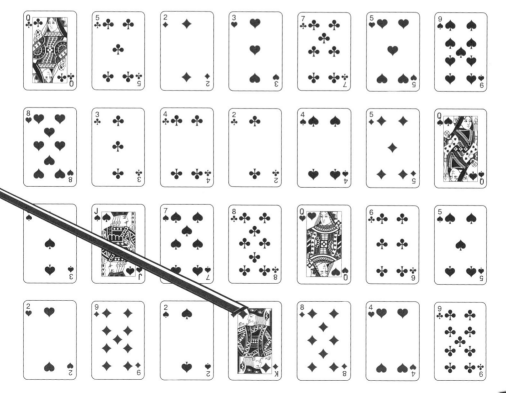

KING ALBERT

*This demanding patience game is simple to play ...
unfortunately, winning is not quite so straightforward.*

AIM OF THE GAME:
In common with many patience games, the aim is to take the
cards from the starting layout and build them into four complete
suit-based foundation piles; just like Klondike (see page 12) but
with rather more scope to go wrong.

LAYOUT

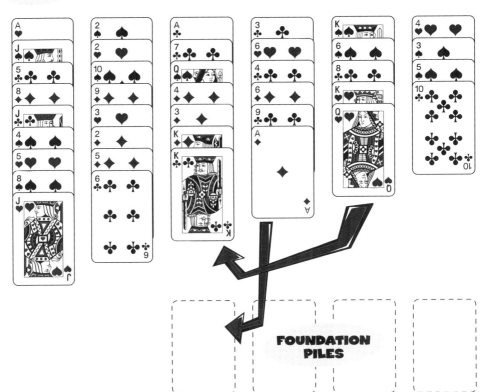

**FOUNDATION
PILES**

TO START

1. Shuffle the pack and deal out 45 cards in rows of nine cards, then eight, seven and so on, down to a single card. The cards should be placed overlapping and face up on a table or board.

2. You should have seven cards left (if you haven't, you've either lost some cards or you're not very good at counting). The seven cards in hand are your 'reserve' and should be placed face up on the board. That's the easy bit done …

HOW TO PLAY

1. Your first objective is to release the Aces from the layout and establish your foundation piles; to do this, you must move other cards out of the way and onto other columns or foundation piles.

2. You can only move cards onto other columns in descending sequences of alternating colour, and you can only move single cards or complete columns – nothing in between.

3. If you move an entire column, you will be left with a gap in your layout which can be filled with any active card. This is a critical part of the game as your decision on which card to move may have a profound impact upon the shape of the game.

4. The seven reserve cards are used for building on the foundations or for 'packing' on the exposed cards in the layout. The reserve cards are a critical part of King Albert, providing the player with the chance to get things moving if the game stalls.

WHEN HAVE YOU WON?

Victory is yours when you've managed to build complete suits of 13 cards on each of the foundation piles. Enjoy the smug, warm glow of triumph as you place the final King on the last foundation pile … it won't happen too often.

RESERVE

DECISIONS, DECISIONS

The use of the reserve cards and the fact that all cards are exposed (face up) throughout reduces the element of chance in King Albert as compared to many other patience games. Study the cards and consider your decisions very carefully. Moving a King to a vacant column in the layout, for example, may seem like a logical action, but sometimes it is better to move a much lower card which will help you open up further columns in less time.

DEMON

OR FASCINATION, THIRTEEN, CANFIELD

AGES: 12+

SKILL LEVEL: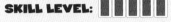

GOOD FOR: Patience prodigies and those in need of a real challenge.

Demon is a demanding game that calls for concentration in abundance and a large helping of brainpower.

AIM OF THE GAME:
To build the cards in suit onto foundation cards ... sounds simple.

TO START

1. Deal 13 cards from a well-shuffled deck into a stack. The cards are placed face down on the table and become 'the heel'. The top card of the heel is turned over.

2. To the right of the heel, deal out one card to establish the foundation card for the hand. Unlike many patience games, Demon does not use Aces or Kings as its foundations but instead uses this variable card which is defined by the deal. Cards are built onto the foundations in ascending order and go 'round the corner'; so, for example, if the foundation card is a three, players must next play a four onto it, then a five and so on. They carry on building upwards until they get to the King, then complete the suit by playing the Ace and, lastly, the two.

3. Finally, deal out four face-up cards from the deck beneath the foundation row to start the layout.

HOW TO PLAY

1. Start by seeing if any of the cards in the layout can either be built onto the foundations or onto one another. Single cards can be moved from the bottom of one column providing they are of alternating colour and descending sequence to the bottom card of the column they join. Entire columns can also be moved, but fragments of columns cannot.

2. Any spaces made in the layout must be immediately filled by the top card from the heel. Once a card has been played from the heel, the next card in line is turned over. When the heel is exhausted, players may fill gaps in the layout from the waste pile (see opposite) but they are no longer obliged to fill these gaps immediately and can, instead, wait for an opportune moment or card.

3. The remaining undealt 34 cards form a stock, which is held in hand. The stock is dealt to a waste pile three cards at a time, although at the end of the deal you may find there are fewer than three cards, in which case you should turn the cards one by one. Cards from the stock can be played either onto the foundation cards or onto the layout. The stock is dealt and re-dealt until either the game is won or becomes blocked.

WHEN HAVE YOU WON?

The object of the game is to play all the cards from the stock and the heel onto the foundation cards. When you have built all 52 cards onto the foundations, you've won. However, be warned – this game is far from easy and it make take you many deals before you make it 'out'.

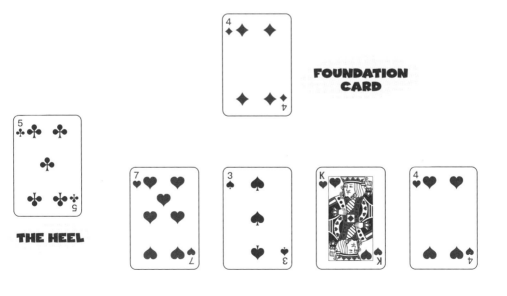

FOUNDATION CARD

THE HEEL

WINNING WAY

Many youngsters will struggle initially to summon up the powers of concentration needed to succeed at Demon. However, you should encourage them to persevere and, most importantly, to take their time. Only by checking each card carefully against both the layout and the foundations do you stand any chance of success.

THE HEEL

As soon as a card of the same rank as the first foundation card appears, it should be moved to the foundation and replaced with the top card of the heel. The next card in the heel is then turned face up.

THE STOCK

GAMES FOR ONE

STOREHOUSE
OR RESERVE

AGES: 10+

SKILL LEVEL: ▌▌▌

GOOD FOR: Younger children who have watched their older siblings playing Demon.

This Demon variant is recommended for children not yet ready for the rigours of the more demanding original.

AIM OF THE GAME:

To build the cards in suit onto Aces, which are placed at the top of the layout as foundation cards.

HOW TO PLAY

Storehouse employs the same rules and layout as Demon (see page 26), but with one exception. Instead of a random card being used to determine the foundation cards, the four Aces are used. Prior to the deal, these cards are withdrawn and placed at the top of the layout.

THE HEEL

FOUNDATION PILES

LAYOUT

GAMES FOR TWO

SNAP!

AGES: 3+

SKILL LEVEL: ▌

GOOD FOR: Exuberant youngsters and anybody who wants a simple, non-strategic but competitive game of cards.

Simple, fast and noisy... the perfect card game for young ones.

AIM OF THE GAME:
To collect all your opponent's cards.

TO START

1. Shuffle a standard 52-card deck and deal out all the cards between the two players. Alternatively, if you don't want to take the time to deal, you can simply cut the cards into two similarly sized stacks. Snap! is hardly a game of science, so it doesn't matter if one player has a few more cards than his or her opponent … although it is probably wise to make sure that the youngest player gets the better of any inequity in the deal (otherwise you'll never hear the last of it).

HOW TO PLAY

1. Players hold their cards (face down) in their hand. The game begins when both players simultaneously turn over their top cards and place them on the table face up in front of them.

LEARNING THE GAME

You can, of course, buy special packs of themed cards especially designed for children to play Snap! with, but it is better to encourage youngsters to play the game with a standard deck. Caricatured images of donkeys, policemen and buses are all very amusing, but they won't teach your children anything about playing cards. By playing Snap! with a 52-card deck, youngsters learn the value of each card and also become familiar with the suits.

WINNING WAY

There are no tactics involved in Snap! To improve their chances of winning, players could follow a strict programme of exercises to improve their reaction times to visual stimuli, but this would, of course, be a little over the top, even for the most competitive of card sharps. The only sound advice that can be given is to play for fun and accept that you will win as many games as you lose.

2. If the two cards revealed are of different values, the two players each turn over the next card in their stack (placing it on top of the previously played card) as before. The game continues in this way until cards of equal value appear together. Upon sight of a matching pair, the players must shout 'Snap!' The first player to utter the word takes their opponent's cards.

CHANGING THE STYLE

Younger players often struggle to master the concept of playing cards simultaneously and their hesitancy can often lead to allegations of cheating, scuffling and (worst of all) snivelling. If you have this problem, an alternative way of playing can be employed. Players simply play their cards alternately onto a central waste pile and shout 'Snap!' when the card played matches the value of the one on top of the pile.

WHO'S THE WINNER?

The person who snaps up all the cards and sits smugly with a hand full of 52 cards is the winner. The loser is the player complaining passionately that he or she has been cheated. An adjudicator may be required in cases of extreme controversy.

MORE PLAYERS

If you want to play Snap! with three or more players, you will need to use two decks of cards. The rules remain the same; just make sure that you properly shuffle all 104 cards.

BEAT MY NEIGHBOUR OUT OF DOORS

OR JACK OUT OF TOWN, STRIP JACK NAKED, BEGGAR MY NEIGHBOUR

AGES: 6+

SKILL LEVEL: ▊

GOOD FOR: Youngsters who want an instantly playable game that will keep them occupied for hours.

It may be a game of chance that requires little tactical thought, but Beat My Neighbour Out of Doors is an extremely valuable game, teaching children to recognize and distinguish between cards of different rank, while also honing their powers of concentration.

AIM OF THE GAME:
To win all 52 cards and leave your opponent empty-handed.

GAMES FOR TWO

TO START

1. A standard 52-card deck is shuffled and dealt between the two players so that each has half the pack.

2. The players hold their cards in a face-down stack; discourage them from trying to fan them as this will only end in disaster.

HOW TO PLAY

1. The non-dealer starts the game, turning over the top card of his or her stack and placing it in the middle of the table.

2. The rank of card played determines how many cards the next player must lay. If the card was a numbered pip card, the second player need only lay one of his or her cards. However, if the card was a 'pay card' (that is to say, either an Ace or a court card), he or she must lay the following cards in compensation:

FOR AN ACE – four pip cards
FOR A KING – three pip cards
FOR A QUEEN – two pip cards
FOR A JACK – one pip card

VOID PAY CARD

PAY CARD

COMPENSATION CARD

3. When payment is complete, the player who laid the pay card collects up the cards from the waste pile and adds them to his or her hand. They then restart the play by laying another card in the centre of the table as before.

4. Frequently, however, a player will turn up a pay card when they are in the midst of paying their opponent for a card. When this happens, the earlier pay card is void and the previously smug opponent must compensate the other player. For example, John puts down a King and Barry begins paying him, turning over a four, a five and then a Jack. The appearance of the Jack means that John must now compensate Barry by putting

down one card. He plays a five and Barry collects the cards from the waste pile and restarts the game.

5. Jacks are the most valuable cards as they give you the chance to win the waste pile while offering only a minimal chance that your opponent will turn up a pay card in the midst of their compensation.

WHO'S THE WINNER?

The winner is the player who collects all the cards, leaving their opponent with none. However, this situation can take hours, days or weeks to achieve. In many cases, it is the player who gives up last who wins the game by default!

HOW TO WIN AT ALL COSTS

This truly is a game of chance; there are no tactics and no strategies that can help you win. In the absence of supernatural intervention, we can only recommend that a player desperate to win invests in an identical pack of cards and simply extracts the Jacks from the deck in readiness to play them at an opportune moment. Of course, that would be cheating ... and that would be very wrong.

GOPS

AGES: 6+

SKILL LEVEL: ▊▊

GOOD FOR: Decisive kids who can think quickly.

Simple rules and an easy set-up make GOPS a popular game with younger children, while its strategic qualities hold the interest of older players. Definitely one for all the siblings.

AIM OF THE GAME:
To outscore your opponents over 13 hands.

TO START

1. Separate a standard 52-card pack into its four suits.

2. Player One is given the 13 club cards and Player Two takes the diamonds. The 13 hearts are put to one side, and the 13 spades are shuffled and placed face down in the middle of the playing table.

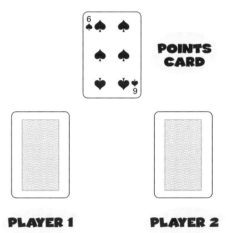

POINTS CARD

PLAYER 1   PLAYER 2

ADD MORE PLAYERS FOR MORE FUN

A three-player version of GOPS can be played by simply including the discarded set of 13 hearts cards in the game. Player Three is given the hearts and joins the game as before. The only other modification required is that if all three players bid with cards of equal value, the points for the hand are now shared three ways.

HOW TO PLAY

1. The deck of spades are called the points cards and to kick off the game the top card is turned over by Player One. The two players must now bid to win the card that has been revealed. If they win it, the points value of the card is added to their score (Ace = 1; Jack, Queen, King = 11, 12 and 13 respectively).

2. The players bid with the cards they hold in hand and can put down any card at any time. All they must do to win is put down a card of higher value than their opponent. Ideally, they must try to put down a card with a value of only one more than that which their rival plays.

3. The two players place the card they wish to play face down in front of them before simultaneously revealing them. That way there can be no cheating or hesitating to gain an advantage.

4. The player who plays the highest card wins the hand and claims the value of the point card (spades) to his or her score. If the two players put down cards of equal value, they each take half the value of the point card.

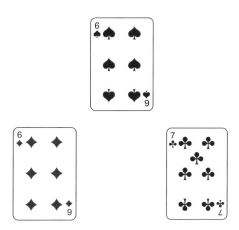

Player Two wins this hand

5. Once a hand has been played, the three cards used are discarded. The second player now turns over a points card and the game continues for a maximum of 13 hands.

WHO'S THE WINNER?

The first player to reach or exceed 46 points has an unassailable lead and is the winner. Keep a written running total of your scores and make sure that each player agrees with what has been recorded. Disagreement over scores can lead to abandoned games, arguments and family feuds. Be warned!

WINNING WAY

Impulsive youngsters can enjoy reasonable success by simply playing high cards to win high cards and vice versa. Of course, that approach will not always work and teenagers may want to think more strategically about their GOPS playing. The game itself takes its name from an acronym which stands for Game Of Pure Strategy, and there are many pages of theory about tactics for GOPS that can be found on the Internet. Unfortunately, these complicated algebraic ramblings, complete with Greek characters and probability symbols, make for impenetrable reading to anybody who has not taken the trouble to get a mathematics doctorate.

WAR

AGES: 6+

SKILL LEVEL: ▮▮

GOOD FOR: Graduates of Snap!

The name alone will get boys queuing up for a game, while War's instant playability should appeal to even the most pacifist of females.

AIM OF THE GAME:
To win all your opponent's cards.

TO START

1. Shuffle a standard 52-card pack and deal out all the cards between the two players.

2. Players do not look at their cards, which are placed face down in a pack in front of them. They are now on the brink of War.

HOW TO PLAY

1. Both players simultaneously turn over the top card in their respective piles and place it face up in the middle of the table.

2. The highest-rank card wins the hand and collects the cards, placing them face down at the bottom of his or her pack. Aces are high and suits are ignored.

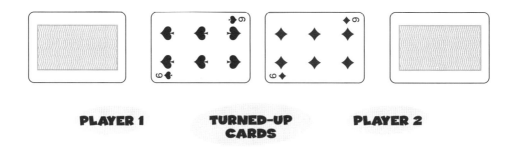

PLAYER 1   **TURNED-UP CARDS**   **PLAYER 2**

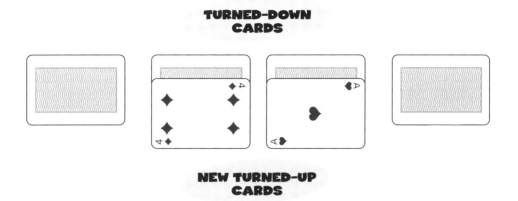

**NEW TURNED-UP
CARDS**

3. If the two cards played are of equal value, the two players must now go to War. They both now place the top cards of their packs face down in the middle of the table. These cards are not revealed; instead, the players return to their packs and take the new top card, turning it over and placing it face up on the table.

4. Whoever plays the highest card wins the hand and collects all six cards from the middle of the table, which are placed face down at the bottom of his or her pack.

5. If, however, the turned-up cards are of equal value, the War continues. Each player puts down another face-down card before turning over the next card in their stack.

6. Should a player run out of cards during a War, the game comes to an end.

WHO'S THE WINNER?

Just like Snap!, the winner is the person who collects all 52 cards, leaving their opponent with nothing. It can take quite some time for the game to reach a conclusion … but that's not necessarily a bad thing.

REFERENCE FOR YOUNGER CHILDREN

War is the perfect game to help your children understand and remember the traditional ranking system for playing cards. Each hand requires the players to make a decision about whether one card is higher than another, so after three or four games they should soon start picking things up. To help them get started, you might want to make them a simple reference chart, which will also help to prevent too many noisy arguments about whether a Jack is higher than an Ace. All you need to do is arrange a suit of cards in order and stick them to a piece of cardboard, or simply write down the following sequence on a piece of paper:

(HIGHEST) **A K Q J 10 9 8 7 6 5 4 3 2** (LOWEST)

SUM

AGES: 6+

SKILL LEVEL: ▮▮

GOOD FOR: Developing your child's mental arithmetic while playing cards.

A game that encourages and rewards attacking play while at the same time challenging your child's maths skills has got to be a good thing ... especially if it keeps them quiet for an hour or two.

AIM OF THE GAME:
To win cards from the layout by matching their sole or collective value to a card held in hand.

TO START

1. Deal out 11 cards to each player and play six cards to the middle of the table, face up and in a row.

HOW TO PLAY

1. The non-dealer leads off and can take from the table any card they can match with one held in hand. So, for example, they can play a King to take another King from the table. Alternatively, they can take more than one card if their collective value is equal to the card they played. So, for example, they could play a King to take a four and a six or even a pair of threes and a four (court cards are all worth ten).

2. The cards won by a player during his or her turn are placed face down in a stack, which is put to one side until the scores are settled at the end of the game.

3. If a player is unable to take any cards during their turn, they must instead discard one of the cards held in hand. The discarded card is added to the face-up row in the middle of the table. Similarly, if there are no cards left to take, the player whose turn it is must play one of their own cards to the table.

4. When the players have no cards left, the remainder of the deck is dealt out and the game resumes. The game continues as before until the cards run dry.

GAMES FOR TWO

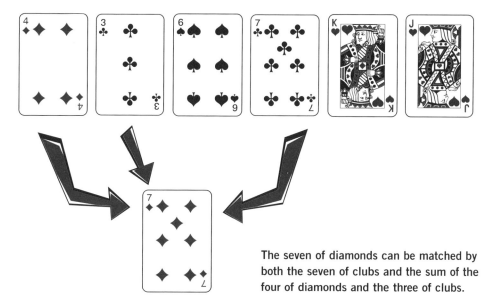

The seven of diamonds can be matched by both the seven of clubs and the sum of the four of diamonds and the three of clubs.

WHO'S THE WINNER?

At the end of the game the players turn over the stack of cards won and total up their scores. Pip cards count one, with court cards and Aces counting two. Ten bonus points are awarded to the player who has won the most cards and five bonus points are awarded for every seven points won by each player.

WINNING WAY

The ten bonus points won by the player claiming the most cards is critical, so players should be encouraged to take multiple cards. A court card that claims a card of equal rank will net you two points, but if you can take three or four lower-rank cards, you will be better off as you will earn a point for each. This strategy will also provide the greatest opportunity for children to test their powers of mental arithmetic.

EIGHTS

OR SWITCH, FAT LADIES

AGES: 8+

SKILL LEVEL: ▌▌ ▌▌

GOOD FOR: Tactical types and those who simply want an instantly playable head-to-head game.

Eights is a quickfire game that is sometimes played impulsively, sometimes strategically, but always enthusiastically.

AIM OF THE GAME:
To get rid of your seven cards before your opponent empties their hand.

TO START

1. Shuffle a 52-card deck and deal out seven cards (one at a time) to both of the players.

2. The remaining cards are placed in a stock pile in the middle of the table, and the top card is turned over to become the game's starter card.

HOW TO PLAY

1. The basic gameplay in Eights is a little like many patience games – you play the cards from your hand onto a pile, building on the active card either in rank or suit.

2. The non-dealer plays first and must try to play a card from their hand onto the starter card. The card laid down must match either in suit or rank, so, for example, a seven of any suit or a club of any rank could be played onto a seven of clubs.

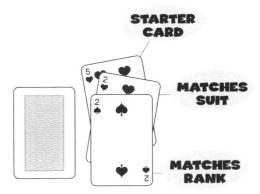

STARTER CARD

MATCHES SUIT

MATCHES RANK

3. If a player does not have a playable card, they must take the top card of the stock pile and add that to their hand; if they still cannot play, they draw cards one at a time from the stock pile until they can.

4. Once a player has laid down a card, the turn passes to their opponent.

GAMES FOR TWO

COMPETITIVE SCORING

For a more competitive form of Eights, which is suitable for teenagers, you can employ an aggregate scoring system over a series of games. The objective in this version of the game is to avoid reaching the critical score of 100 debit points; the player who reaches this total first is the loser. Points are awarded to each player in respect of the cards they are left holding at the end of each hand. Different points are awarded for each card as follows:

EIGHTs = 50 points
KING, QUEEN OR JACK = 10 points
ACE = 1 point
CARDS TWO-TEN = 2–10 points respectively

If the game ends in a block, each player is debited the value of the cards held in hand. Of course, a player who wins a game outright has no addition to their score.

5. If the stock pile becomes exhausted, a player unable to take their turn simply has to pass.

6. Even if a player is able to play a card from their hand, they may still elect to first take a card from the stock pile. They must, however, eventually play a card, as players cannot pass while holding a playable card.

7. 'So,' you're thinking, 'why is this game called Eights?' I was coming to that bit. In this game, eights are wild cards and can be played at any time onto any card. Players can elect to play an eight even if they have another playable card. When playing an eight, you must specify which suit it

represents to clarify whether the previous suit continues or whether you wish to change to another suit (you have free choice). However, though the suit of an eight is wild, the rank is not. The next card played must either be another eight or a card that matches the stipulated suit.

WHO'S THE WINNER?

The first player to get rid of all the cards in their hand is the winner. If, however, and as often happens, the game becomes blocked and neither player can make a move, there has to be a count-up to determine the winner. The player with the fewest cards is the winner.

SPIT
OR SPEED

AGES: 9+

SKILL LEVEL: ▌▌▌

GOOD FOR: Competitive siblings with quick brains and even quicker hands.

AIM OF THE GAME:
To move all the 15 cards out of your layout before your opponent empties theirs.

TO START

1. Shuffle a standard 52-card deck and deal out the cards equally between the two players, who should be seated opposite one another at a table.

2. Each player must now deal 15 of their own cards into a 'patience'-style layout. The cards are placed in five stock piles: the first contains one card, the second two … down to the fifth pile of five cards. The cards are set face down, with the exception of the bottom card in each pile, which is turned over.

3. The remaining 11 cards are the spit cards and they are held face down in a pile in the player's hand. Players are not allowed to look at the spit cards in advance of them being played.

HOW TO PLAY

1. When both players are ready to play, they each turn over their top spit card and place it in the middle of the table (between the two layouts).

2. The game, which begins as soon as the two cards are turned over, is played like a rapidfire version of patience. The basic objective is to play all your cards out of your layout and onto the spit piles.

3. Players play continuously (they do not take consecutive turns) and continue until they can make no more moves.

4. Cards are played from the bottom of the stock piles in the layout onto either of the two spit piles and turned face up. A card moved to a spit pile must be the next in sequence (either up or down), irrespective of suit.

5. Players are only allowed to use one hand to move their cards and can only play one card at a time.

6. As cards are played from the layout, the bottom card in each stock pile is turned over. If a stock pile is emptied, the gap in the layout can be filled by moving the bottom card of another stock pile into the space.

SPIT CARDS IN HAND

TURNED-UP SPIT CARDS

SPIT CARDS IN HAND

7. As soon as a card touches a spit pile or a space in the layout, it is deemed to have been played. There is no going back, and as soon as the card touches down, your opponent is free to play onto it.

8. When neither player can make any more moves, both shout 'Spit!' and turn over the top cards from the spit cards held in hand. The two cards are placed on top of the respective spit piles and play resumes.

WHO'S THE WINNER?

The first player to empty the cards from their layout onto the spit piles is the undisputed Spit king. However, if the game reaches stalemate and neither player can make any further moves, the game can either be considered drawn or, if you are determined to get a positive result, you can count up the cards each player has left in their layouts, awarding victory to whoever has fewest.

COLONEL

AGES: 9+

SKILL LEVEL: ▮▮▮

GOOD FOR: Rummy graduates looking for a fresh challenge.

A compulsive and addictive Rummy variant (see page 62), which will have the noisiest of teenagers enraptured.

AIM OF THE GAME:
To meld a hand of ten cards into sets of three or four,
either by sequence or rank.

TO START

1. Both players are dealt out ten cards, which are placed face down in front of them.

2. The remainder of the cards are placed face down in a neat stock pile in the centre of the table and the top card is turned over and placed to one side. This aspect of the game (and much of the gameplay) is identical to Rummy (see page 62).

HOW TO PLAY

1. The non-dealer leads off and can take either the exposed face-up card (which is called the option card) or the unseen top card from the stock pile. Whichever they choose, they must then discard one of their cards, which is placed face up and becomes the new option card.

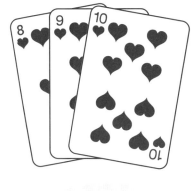

SEQUENCE

THREE-OF-A-KIND

GAMES FOR TWO

RISING TO THE CHALLENGE

An optional twist on Colonel sees the introduction of a challenge. At any point during the game prior to the stock pile running out, one of the players can challenge their opponent to put down their cards and have a count-up. If the player challenged declines, the game continues as normal; however, if they accept, play is brought to a halt and the cards are scored in the same way as when the stock pile runs out.

SCORING

Colonel can be played on a game-by-game basis, with the first to win a set number of hands declared the champion, or it can be played using a more complicated but traditional points system. In the latter scenario, the winning player receives points commensurate with the difference between the value of the cards held at the end of the game compared to their opponent's closing hand. So, for example, if Tom holds two Kings (value = 20) when the stock runs out but Joe has two Queens and a Jack (value = 30 points), Tom wins the game and adds the score of ten (30 – 20 = 10) to his total. The first player to reach an agreed figure is the champion.

2. At the end of their turn the player may now declare any sequences or sets of cards they have completed. They do not have to do this, but should they want to, the sets are placed face up on the table.

3. Either player can add to a declared three-of-a-kind or sequence during the game, provided they do so during their turn. So, for example, if Tom declares three Kings during his turn, his opponent, Joe, can lay off the odd King he holds when it is his turn.

4. Players take turns alternately, with each free to take either the stock or option card.

WHO'S THE WINNER?

The first player to empty their hand and play out all their cards is the winner. Of course, this situation does not always arise, so if the stock pile is emptied before either player can play out their cards, the game is decided on points. The players count up the value of the cards held in hand, with court cards and Aces counting ten and all others the value of their pips. The player with the lowest total is the winner.

WINNING WAY

As in Rummy, the key to success is to keep your options open for as long as possible and to note the cards collected and ignored by your opponent. Avoid pursuing sets that can be completed by only one card, and instead go after those that offer a greater probability of success.

WHIST
OR TRUMPS

AGES: 9+

SKILL LEVEL: ▌▌▌▌▌

GOOD FOR: Teenagers who want to develop their card-playing skills and enjoy a competitive game.

Whist is a great introduction to the world of serious grown-up card games and opens up a catalogue of games to the budding card player.

AIM OF THE GAME:
To win more tricks than your opponents.

TO START

Whist is a serious game and young players must be taught to respect the rules of the game. It may seem stuffy to start dictating how the cards are to be shuffled, cut and dealt, but if you can establish good habits now, you will avoid confusion in the future.

1. To determine who deals first, the players must cut the pack. The cards are placed in the centre of the table and each player in turn lifts off a small section from the deck. The card at the bottom of each section is shown to the other players and the player who has 'cut' the highest card (Aces are high) deals first. Should two players draw cards of equal rank, a second cut is made. The job of dealer passes around the table in a clockwise fashion with each hand.

2. The dealer shuffles the cards and passes them to the player on their left, who cuts the deck and places the bottom half of the pack on the top half. The cards can now be dealt.

3. Cards are dealt one at a time and are placed face down in front of each player. The first card is dealt to the player on the left of the dealer, who works his or her way clockwise around the table.

HOW TO PLAY
(TWO-PLAYER WHIST)

1. Each player is dealt seven cards.

2. Player Two starts the game, and the game continues, as explained in The Lead. The winner of each trick is ticked in the diagram to the right.

WHO'S THE WINNER?

The first player to win four tricks is the winner. Player One triumphs here, winning four tricks to his or her opponent's three.

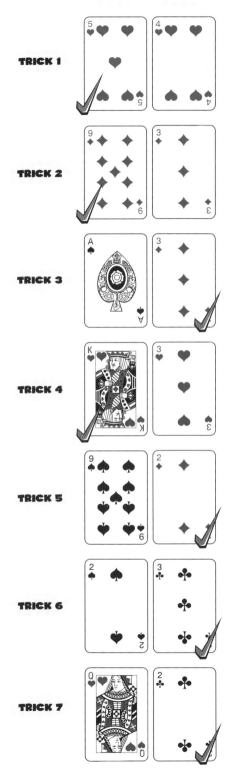

PLAYER 1 PLAYER 2

TRICK 1

TRICK 2

TRICK 3

TRICK 4

TRICK 5

TRICK 6

TRICK 7

DEFINITIONS

TRICKS

A trick is the name given to one complete round of Whist; so, for example, if you have four players, the four cards on the table at the end of a round constitute a trick. The highest card played wins the trick and the victorious player gets to keep the cards, which will be counted up at the end to determine the game's winner.

THE LEAD

The player to the left of the dealer starts the game and lays down a card face up on the table. The card chosen is the lead card and the other players must follow its suit if they can. If the lead card had been a six of diamonds, the next player must play a diamond if they have one. To stand a chance of winning the hand, he or she must play a diamond card of higher rank than the six their opponent played. If they have no diamonds, they cannot 'follow' and must instead 'discard' a card of a different suit. You cannot win a trick with a discarded card, so its rank is irrelevant.

TRUMPS

Many Whist variants employ trump cards which can be used when a player is unable to follow suit. A trump will beat any other card except a trump of higher rank. The trump suit is defined by an extra cut of the deck prior to dealing.

49

GERMAN WHIST

AGES: 9+

SKILL LEVEL: ▌▌▌▌

GOOD FOR: Tactical types with time on their hands.

German Whist is a game that calls for concentration, rigour and strategy. Impulsive younger siblings should resist the temptation to join in unless they are blessed with the tactical brain of a military commander.

AIM OF THE GAME:
To win seven of the last 13 tricks.

TO START

1. Thirteen cards are dealt to each player. The remaining cards are placed in a stock pile on the table and the dealer turns over the top card to reveal the trump suit for the game. This card is also the prize for the first trick winner.

  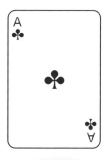 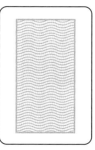

TRUMPS

HOW TO PLAY

1. The non-dealer leads off the first trick and the usual rules apply. The next player must follow suit or, if he or she can't, must play a trump. If they can do neither, they knock on the table, surrender one of their cards and lose the trick. The two cards played are put to one side and will not feature in the remainder of the game.

2. The winner of the trick collects the face-up card (remember the card we turned over to set the trump suit), while the loser takes the top card from the face-down stack. The next card in the stack is turned over and is the prize for the winner of the next trick.

3. Trick winners lead each subsequent hand and the game continues in this fashion until the stack of cards is exhausted. No scores are kept for this phase of the game, as the aim is to mould and strengthen your hand in readiness for the game's second phase, which now commences.

4. The trick playing continues, but with the stock pile gone, the players' hand of cards now diminishes with each trick. Scores are kept, with players receiving a point for each winning trick.

WHO'S THE WINNER?

The first player to win seven tricks in the second phase of the game is the winner.

TRICKY TRICKS

Strictly speaking, you must follow suit if you can and, if you can't, you must play a trump if you have one. However, if the card on offer to the trick winner is worthless, you may not want to sacrifice a more valuable and higher ranking card, in which case you must forget that you've got a playable card. Knock on the table, surrender another card and take the face-down card instead. Should you later need to use the card, you'll have to tell your opponent it was the one you picked up upon losing the earlier trick. Of course, you're only cheating yourself ... but then, as they say, all's fair in love and Whist.

WINNING WAY

German Whist is effectively a game of two halves. The first half sees the players attempt to engineer the best hand possible by winning (or in some cases losing) tricks; while the second half sees them go all out to secure the seven trick wins that will bring ultimate victory. In the first half of the game, it is important for players to think very carefully about whether they want to win particular tricks or not. The exposed card is your prize for victory, and you must decide if you want it or not. Decide how good a card it is worth playing to win the exposed card. In some cases, you are better off taking your chance with the face-down card!

GAMES FOR TWO OR MORE

PAIRS
OR CONCENTRATION, MEMORY, PELMANISM

AGES: 3+

SKILL LEVEL: ▌▌

GOOD FOR: Getting competitive youngsters to concentrate and test their powers of memory.

As simple as Snap! but with less noise, Pairs is the perfect way to get youngsters using their brains rather than their mouths.

AIM OF THE GAME:
To locate matching pairs and collect more cards than your opponents by the time the table is bare.

TO START

1. For this game to run smoothly, it is imperative that the cards are laid out properly at the start of the game. The cards (which must be shuffled) are placed face down on a flat surface (for example, a table) and spaced evenly in a grid made up of 13 rows of four cards.

HOW TO PLAY

1. The game begins when the youngest player turns over two cards in the layout. If the cards revealed are of equal value, the player picks them up and puts them to one side. He or she may now reveal another pair of cards, and their turn continues until they choose two cards that do not match.

2. When two unmatched cards are revealed, they remain in the layout and are turned face down once more before the next player takes their turn.

3. It is important that players take great care not to make a mess of the layout. If cards move out of line and start overlapping, the game can easily descend into chaos.

4. Players take alternate turns until there are no cards left to play.

WHO'S THE WINNER?

At the end of the game players count up how many pairs of cards they have each collected. The player with the most cards is the winner.

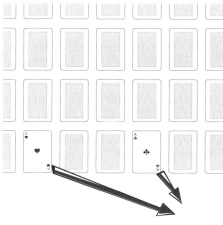

TOO EASY

If matching cards by their face value becomes too easy, you can also make the game colour-specific. So, for example, if you reveal the two of hearts, you will only complete a match if you locate the two of diamonds next.

WINNING WAY

Pairs is essentially a game that tests players' ability to memorize card positions. To improve your chances of winning, you must endeavour to employ strategies that will help you recall the positions of the cards revealed throughout the game. Some people use repetition, chanting to themselves as if they were saying a mantra (for example, 'top left Ace, bottom right Queen'), while others try to visualize the cards they have seen. More sophisticated memory systems like 'chunking' can be researched through self-help books if you're feeling very competitive. Be warned, though – children often have very good memories compared to those found in the addled brains of adults. If you're not careful, your precocious six-year-old might well give you a sound thrashing at Pairs.

CARDGO
OR BINGO, BANGO

AGES: 5+

SKILL LEVEL: ▮

GOOD FOR: Noisy parties and prize-chasing children.

A card game that harnesses the inexplicable addictiveness of bingo and the opportunity to win prizes is irresistible for any pre-teen partygoer.

AIM OF THE GAME:
To get rid of your cards while there are prizes still to be won!

TO START

1. This is definitely a game that requires supervision, so appoint a responsible adult to act as dealer and game caller.

2. Once the dealer has all the players seated around a table, he or she deals five cards to each of them and places the remainder of the pack face down at his or her side.

3. Each player holds his or her five cards in their hand and well away from the glare of nosey opponents.

DEALER'S CARD

PLAYER'S HAND

HOW TO PLAY

1. The game begins when the dealer turns over the top card of his or her stack and announces its value; so, for example, if the top card is a four of diamonds, they will simply say 'Four'. The dealer continues to turn the cards over, announcing them at a steady and unbroken pace until the game reaches its end.

2. The players check each newly revealed card against those they hold in hand. If they have a card of matching value, they must place it face down in front of them.

3. The flow of the game must be continuous; make it clear to the players that if they are distracted and miss a card, you will not hold the game up for them to backtrack. Concentration is the essence of this game.

WHO'S THE WINNER?

The winner is the first player to turn all their cards face down. When this feat is achieved, the victorious player must shout 'Cardgo'. If two players put their cards down at the same time, it is the first to call 'Cardgo' who wins the game.

NO ARGUMENTS

It is not that likely to happen, but to avoid squabbles breaking out, the dealer needs to make it clear in advance whether two cards of the same rank can be played at the same time or not if a player happens to hold more than one of them.

SUITS IN THE HOUSE

If you want to get specific and make things a little harder, you can play the game with a divided pack. Simply split the pack by colour, separating the red cards from the black. Deal the reds to the players and keep the black cards as the stock. If you have more than five players, you will need two packs of cards.

CHEAT

AGES: 5+

SKILL LEVEL: ▊▊

GOOD FOR: Ensuring your card playing descends into a chaotic, sometimes hilarious, but always deafening occasion.

With minimal rules and scope to bluff, cheat, shout and accuse, this is the perfect game with which to kick off the card playing at any family gathering.

AIM OF THE GAME:

To get rid of all your cards using a combination of bluff and brains.

TO START

1. Get all the players seated around a table, spacing them carefully to make sure cards are out of view and opponents out of reach of each other. If you have more than four players, you may like to use two decks of cards shuffled together.

2. The players pick a card from the deck. The person with the lowest card is the dealer, who then distributes the entire deck between the players as evenly as possible. Cards are dealt individually and face down.

CHEATS PROSPER

Try putting down more than the declared amount of cards; so, for example, playing three cards when you say that you're laying two. If you can fool your opponents, you'll soon get rid of your hand. Of course, if they catch you, you'll be forced to pick up all the cards on the table.

HOW TO PLAY

1. The player to the left of the dealer starts the game by placing a card face down in the centre of the table and naming its value. For example, saying 'Four'.

2. The turn now passes around the table in a clockwise direction, and players must build on the previously played card by playing one higher, one lower or the same. So, in our example, Player Two must now lay a card down on top of the four and say 'Three', 'Four' or 'Five'. They can also play more than one card; so, for example, Player Two could say 'Two threes' or 'Three fives'. Of course, they may not have any fives, let alone three of them, but in this game that doesn't necessarily matter. There is no option to pass or take any kind of penalty. If you haven't got a playable card, you simply have to play another card and bluff.

3. If a player suspects that an opponent is bluffing and has laid a card that is not in sequence, he or she can accuse them of cheating. **The accuser shouts 'Cheat' and** the card played is revealed. If the accuser has made a good call, the pile of cards on the table passes to the bluffer as punishment. However, if the call of cheat was wrong and the card played is in sequence, the accuser has to take up all the cards in the centre.

4. After any challenge, whether successful or not, the player who picks up the cards restarts the game.

WHO'S THE WINNER?

The person who gets rid of all his or her cards first is the winner. To find out who comes second and third, turn all the cards over and add up the numbers on your cards. Picture cards count as ten points and an Ace counts as 15 points. The person with the most points is the loser and the person with the least points is second.

GO FISH

AGES: 6+

SKILL LEVEL: ▌▌

GOOD FOR: Cheeky kids.

An uncomplicated gem that will entertain youngsters and encourage a little skulduggery and much excitement.

AIM OF THE GAME:
To collect or steal complete suits of cards ...
and obviously to shout 'Go fish!' at regular intervals.

TO START

1. The game requires 3–6 players (who should be seated) and a standard 52-card deck.

2. Each player is dealt five cards and the remaining cards are set on the table in a face-down stock.

HOW TO PLAY

1. The player to the dealer's left (let's call him Arthur) takes the first turn. He asks a specific player for a particular rank (though not suit) of card; for example, 'Martha, give me your Kings'. Arthur can only ask Martha for a rank of card that he already owns (so he can only ask for Kings if he holds a King).

2. If Martha has any Kings, she must hand them all over to Arthur, who then takes another turn. As long as he continues to ask opponents for cards that they have, Arthur continues to have extra turns.

3. When Arthur asks an opponent for a rank of card that they do not hold, the opponent shouts 'Go fish'. Arthur must then take the top card from the stock; if that card is of the rank he asked for, he takes another turn. He must, however, reveal the card to the group before taking another turn.

4. If the card Arthur drew from the stock is not of the rank he had asked for, his turn ends and the game continues with the player who had shouted 'Go fish' then taking a turn.

5. When a player collects a complete set of four cards of the same rank, he or she must show them to the other players and set them face down in front of him or her.

WHO'S THE WINNER?

There are two ways to win a game of 'Go fish' – you can announce your win with a shout of 'Got my wish!' (as in the song lyric, 'Go fish – got my wish!') – and whichever scenario occurs first brings the game to an end:

1. The person who gets rid of all their cards first is the winner (although this does not always happen).

2. The game ends when the stock of cards runs out. The winner is the player who has discarded the most sets of four cards.

WINNING WAY

Examine your cards very carefully; keep them organized in your hand so that you know what you have and what you're seeking to build on. You must also try to make a mental note of the cards your opponents seek. Also, consider keeping quiet about pairs of cards you hold; wait until another player asks for those cards from a third party, thereby revealing that they hold the complementary pair.

TOO EASY

If you want to take the game to its bitter end, you can continue playing even when the stock of cards runs out. The 'Go fish' aspect of the game is no longer applicable, so if you ask a player for a card they don't have, the turn simply passes directly to the player you asked.

RUMMY

AGES: 6+

SKILL LEVEL: ▌▌▌

GOOD FOR: Teaching grandma who's the best at cards.

Rummy is one of the most popular family card games in the world, and with good reason. The rules are simple, the gameplay is slick and victory is always sweet.

AIM OF THE GAME:

To meld your hand into sets of cards that either run sequentially (for example, Jack, Queen, King of hearts) or that are equal in value (for example, three Aces). Alternatively, you can win the game with a run of seven cards (for example, Ace to seven of clubs).

TO START

1. Rummy can be played with 2–7 players. The players cut to deal, with the lowest card determining the dealer.

2. Each player is given seven cards, which are dealt individually and face down. When all players have their seven cards, the dealer gives an eighth card to the player seated to his or her left. The stack of remaining cards in the deck is placed face down in the centre of the table.

HOW TO PLAY

1. The player who has the eight cards starts the game by throwing away one of his or her cards. The discarded card starts a new, face-up pile next to the stack placed in the centre of the table.

2. The turn passes around the table in a clockwise direction. Players now have two options: they can either take the top face-up card or, if that card is not appealing, they can turn over the top card of the face-down stack. Whichever option they choose, they must throw away one card onto the face-up stack at the end of their turn. They can, of course, discard the card they just picked up.

3. The game continues, with players taking alternate turns until either one player declares that they are ready to 'Go down', or the stack of face-down cards runs out. If the latter occurs, the adjacent pile of face-up cards is simply inverted and the game subsequently resumed.

 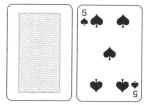

This player has just picked up a third Queen and discarded the five of spades. They should 'go down' immediately.

WHO'S THE WINNER?

1. The winner is the player who is first to successfully assemble his or her hand into sets of complete cards. A set of three plus a set of four (either runs or cards of equal value) is enough to secure victory. So, for example, a trio of Kings plus the seven, eight, nine and ten of hearts would make for a winning hand.

2. To find out who comes second and third, the remaining players must reveal their cards and count up the pip value of any cards that do not form part of complete sets. If, for example, you had a trio of Queens, a pair of twos and a pair of fours, your deficit score for the hand would be 12. The Queens count as a complete set so have a value of zero, but the sum of the other cards, which are not in complete sets, counts against you. The player with the lowest deficit score comes second.

WINNING WAY

The key to success in Rummy lies in pursuing the right cards. Keep your options open for as long as you can; for example, the Ace and two of spades can only make a set of cards if one card (the three of spades) comes up. By contrast, if you hold the four of hearts, the four of clubs and the three of clubs, your chances of making a set are greatly increased as any one of four cards can complete a playable trio.

MIXING UP THE RUMMY

To increase the pace of the game, some slight changes can be made. Firstly, you can introduce jokers to represent any card in a set. Twos are also traditionally used for this purpose. Secondly, you can rule that a run of six cards in sequence is considered a winning hand providing the seventh card has a pip value of seven or less.

OLD MAID

AGES: 6+

SKILL LEVEL:

GOOD FOR: Family gatherings and sedate social occasions.

Pairs with added tension would be a fair description of this time-honoured classic, which has long been beloved by young card players.

AIM OF THE GAME:
To get rid of your cards and avoid
being left holding the old maid.

TO START

1. Remove one Queen from a standard deck to ensure that there is a single 'old maid' left who cannot be paired during the game.

2. The cards are shuffled and all 51 are dealt individually around the table. Unless you have three players, the cards will not divide evenly, so it is likely that some players will have one card more than the others. This inequity should not impact significantly on the game and will be redressed if the deal rotates around the table in the usual fashion with each hand.

3. The players pick up their hand and immediately discard any pairs of cards they hold, putting them face down into the centre of the table.

4. With the completed pairs discarded, each player now fans his or her cards and places them face down on the table.

HOW TO PLAY

1. The dealer goes first, offering his or her cards to the player immediately to their left, who must take one card without seeing it. The player adds the card to their hand and if it completes a pair they can discard the matched cards onto the waste pile. If it is another singleton, they must keep it.

2. The player now fans his or her cards and offers them to their left-hand neighbour who must take one.

3. The game continues in the same way moving around the table in a clockwise direction, with players either discarding pairs or adding to their hand.

WHO'S THE LOSER?

When a player has successfully paired all his or her cards and has emptied their hand, they are safe. Play continues until one player is left with a single card ... the odd Queen or 'old maid'. That player is the loser.

WINNING WAY

This is another game of chance, so there is little point fretting over strategy and tactics. All you can do is make sure that you check your cards carefully for pairs at each turn. If you miss a matching couple and offer your cards to your neighbour, you run the risk of losing that pair. Aside from this precaution, you must watch to see when two of the three Queens are matched. When there is only one Queen left, you must try to avoid her at all costs. If she ends up in your possession, you will have to hope that your neighbour takes her off your hands; in such a situation, you are best advised to place the offending card to either the left or right of centre in your fanned hand. Players rarely take the cards at either end or in the middle. The only other thing you can do is cross your fingers and hope.

DOMINOES
OR SEVENS

AGES: 7+

SKILL LEVEL: ▌▌

GOOD FOR: Numerate youngsters with large tables and a well-honed competitive spirit.

Dominoes offers a rarely found combination of speed and strategy, making it a firm favourite with youngsters eager to move on from more frivolous games of fun and fortune.

AIM OF THE GAME:
Be the first to use up all your cards
by playing them onto the layout.

TO START

1. Cut the cards to select a dealer; the player who draws the lowest card gets the job. The entire deck of 52 cards is distributed as evenly as possible between the players. Any inequity will be redressed providing the deal rotates for each hand.

2. The player to the left of the dealer leads off but must play a seven to start the game. If he or she doesn't have a seven, they must 'knock' and the turn passes around the table in a clockwise direction.

HOW TO PLAY

1. Once a seven has been played, the next player must try to play onto that card and build up the layout. If the game had commenced with the first player laying a seven of diamonds, the next player has three choices: build in sequence, playing the six of diamonds to the left of the seven or the eight to the right; or they can play another seven of a different suit above the opening card.

2. If a player is unable to add to the layout in any direction, he or she must 'knock' and the turn passes on.

3. As the game develops, there will be four rows of cards building to left and right, and players can build on any of these rows in either ascending or descending sequence.

WHO'S THE WINNER?

The first player to get rid of all his or her cards is the winner. Play continues until only one player is left holding cards; that unlucky soul collects the wooden spoon and is the Dominoes dunce.

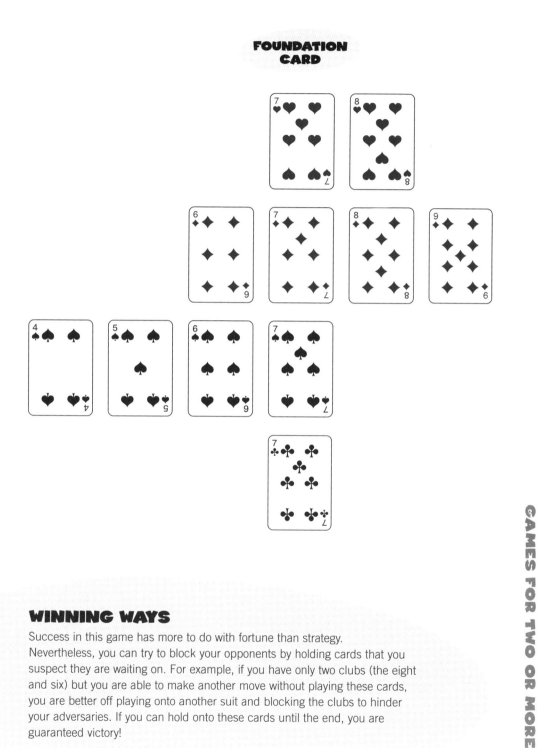

FOUNDATION CARD

WINNING WAYS

Success in this game has more to do with fortune than strategy.
Nevertheless, you can try to block your opponents by holding cards that you
suspect they are waiting on. For example, if you have only two clubs (the eight
and six) but you are able to make another move without playing these cards,
you are better off playing onto another suit and blocking the clubs to hinder
your adversaries. If you can hold onto these cards until the end, you are
guaranteed victory!

GAMES FOR TWO OR MORE

DRY JACK

AGES: 7+

SKILL LEVEL: ▮▮▮

GOOD FOR: Rainy days on holiday and those rare occasions when there's no TV, no stereo and no phone reception.

Dry Jack is another multi-player game that can be played for prizes or for pride ... whichever you choose, it's a great way to while away a few hours.

AIM OF THE GAME:
To win as many scoring cards as you can
and take dry tricks whenever possible.

TO START

1. Cut the cards to select a dealer; the player who draws the lowest card gets the job and deals six cards to each player. If you have more than four players, you will need to use two packs of cards.

2. Four cards are then dealt face up into a neat pile in the centre of the table. The remainder of the deck is put to one side in readiness for the next deal.

PLAYER 1's HAND

STOCK

PLAYER 2's HAND

HOW TO PLAY

1. The player to the left of the dealer leads off and plays a card from his or her hand onto the top of the face-up pile. If they play a card of equal rank, they win the cards beneath. The cards won are put to one side until the end of the game, when the scores are finally settled.

2. If they play a card of another rank onto the face-up pile, the turn simply moves around the table in a clockwise direction.

3. The gameplay is relatively simple and moves quickly from one player to the next. The only complicating factors are that:

Jacks operate like trumps and take the face-up pile irrespective of the value of the top card.

If a player wins a new pile that consists of just one card, that player is said to have completed a 'dry trick' and wins a bonus ten points.

4. When the stock pile is taken, the next player must start a new pile by laying a card face up into the centre of the table.

5. The game continues in this way until the players have each used their six cards. The dealer then deals out another hand of six cards to each and adds four cards to the stock pile.

WHO'S THE WINNER?

The game reaches its end when there are not enough cards left to complete a fresh deal. At this point, the players turn over the cards they have won and points are awarded on the following basis:

THE PLAYER WHO HAS WON THE MOST CARDS – 5
THE PLAYER WHO HAS THE MOST HEARTS – 5
FOR EACH JACK HELD – 1
FOR THE ACE OF SPADES – 2
FOR THE TEN OF SPADES – 2

Don't forget to take into consideration the ten bonus points awarded to any player completing a dry trick.

WINNING WAY

Players must choose very carefully when to make an attack. It would obviously be unwise to forgo the chance to make a dry trick, but in other circumstances you may like to wait before playing a matching card. Jacks, in particular, should be saved up until a scoring card has been played or until there are several hearts in the pile.

I PROMISE
OR 'OH WELL', NOMINATION TRUMPS

AGES: 8+

SKILL LEVEL: ▌▌▌▌

GOOD FOR: Family parties and other mixed gatherings.

Whether played for stakes or fun, I Promise is an engaging trick-based game that is a favourite with kids and adults alike!

AIM OF THE GAME:
To successfully predict how many tricks
you will win in any given deal.

GAMES FOR TWO OR MORE

TO START

1. Cut the cards to select a dealer; the player who draws the lowest card gets the job. The dealer distributes the cards until there are not enough to make another complete round of the table. Each player must have the same number of cards as his or her rivals, with any spare cards put to one side.

2. Before the players look at their cards, the dealer turns over the last card dealt to himself or herself as this card indicates the trump suit for the deal.

3. The players now assess their cards and begin making their 'promises'. The player to the left of the dealer starts the process and must declare how many tricks they 'promise' to win during the hand. The number announced is recorded by the dealer.

HOW TO PLAY

1. When all players have made their predictions, the trick playing begins, with the player sitting to the left of the dealer laying the first card.

2. In the fashion of Whist (see page 48), all players must either follow suit or, if they can't, play a trump. If they can do neither, they discard a card. The player laying the highest trump, or if no trumps are played, the highest card that follows in suit, wins that particular trick.

3. At the end of each trick, the dealer records who won. The trick winner gets to lead off the next trick.

This player could bid three tricks fairly safely.

With only two high cards, this player would be safer bidding two tricks or three if spades or diamonds were trumps.

WHO'S THE WINNER?

Play continues until the cards run out. The scores are then counted up and players are awarded one point for each winning trick, plus a bonus of ten points if they successfully predicted the number of winning tricks they would make. So, for example, if Tom said he'd win three and did so, he'd earn 13 points for the hand, but if Meryl had said she'd win five but only won four, her total would be four points. Players continue playing hands in this way and the first person to reach a total of 100 points is the winner.

WINNING WAY

Avoid reaching your predicted total too early in the hand, as you may find that your opponents gang up on you to ensure you win an additional trick that will mean you lose your ten-point bonus. For example, if you predict you will win three tricks and take the first two of eight, you would be unwise to play a high-ranking trump at the next hand. Sure, you'll take the trick, but with five hands remaining you cannot afford to win any more, and you may find yourself vulnerable should your opponents decide to conspire against you. If they all play low-ranking cards, you may be forced to take an unwanted victory.

I PROMISE NOT TO

Variations on the game include reducing the number of cards by one each time, moving the deal around the table and predicting how many tricks you won't win. In this version, a player has all his or her points deducted for that round if they end up winning the amount of tricks they said that they wouldn't win.

KNOCK-OUT WHIST OR TRUMPS

AGES: 9+

SKILL LEVEL: ▮▮▮▮

GOOD FOR: Kids who think they've mastered Rummy and want to impress with their trick-playing prowess.

Absorbing, tactical and time-consuming, Knock-out Whist is perfect for competitive teenagers with a desire to win.

AIM OF THE GAME:
To survive the early rounds of the game and win the final trick of the final hand.

TO START

1. The gameplay of Knock-out Whist is not greatly different to that described for Two-Player Whist (see page 48). It is, in essence, a simple trick-based game and can be played by up to seven players with a standard deck.

2. After the pack has been cut and the player with the lowest card has been appointed dealer, the players are each dealt seven cards. The remainder of the deck is placed on the table and the dealer turns over the top card to set the trump suit for the hand.

HOW TO PLAY

1. The player to the left of the dealer leads off the first trick and can play any card to start the game.

2. The turn moves around the table clockwise and, in the usual fashion, players follow suit to continue the trick. Alternatively, they can play a trump card, or failing that they must knock on the table to indicate that they cannot play a card onto the trick. The knocking player must then surrender one of his or her cards.

3. The trick is won by the highest trump card (Aces are high) or the highest card that follows suit if no trumps are played. The dealer keeps score along the way, writing down the number of tricks won in each hand by each player.

4. The winner of a trick leads to the next trick, and the winner of the most tricks in a hand gets to choose the trump suit for the next deal.

DOG'S LIFE

The first player knocked out of the game can (if all parties have agreed prior to the game) be granted what is known as a 'dog's life'. They are given a single card at the next deal and can play the card on any trick they choose, so if the other players have six cards, they can pass on five tricks before making their move. If they win the trick, they rejoin the game and are dealt a normal hand on the next deal. If, however, they fail, they are knocked out of the game along with any other players who have failed to win a trick during the round. A further variation that, again, must be agreed by all parties is to provide the first player out with one more chance of staying in the game after failing with the 'dog's life' through a 'blind dog'. Here the player is given a card face down and can choose to play the unseen card on any of the tricks. Though the chances of winning a trick are slim, it's a great feeling to win and get back into the game simply on the turn of a blind card.

5. With each hand the number of cards dealt reduces by one, so the second deal sees each player receive six cards and at the seventh and final deal the players receive just one card each.

6. The knock-out element of the game comes into play at the end of each hand, when any players who have failed to win a trick during that deal are knocked out. These players play no further part in the game.

WHO'S THE WINNER?

The winner is either the player who wins the final trick of the final hand or the last player left when all rivals are eliminated.

WINNING WAY

When choosing trumps, opt for the suit from which you have most cards. If you have equal numbers of cards from two suits, go for the one from which you have lowest-ranking cards. A high-ranked non-trump will still offer a good prospect of victory.

GAMES FOR PARTIES

GO BOOM!
OR ROCKAWAY

AGES: 4+

SKILL LEVEL: ▮▮▮

GOOD FOR: Parties and rowdy get-togethers!

PLAYERS: 4 (more can play, but a second pack of cards is needed)

This classic is a favourite among children and a great introduction to cards for youngsters. But don't be fooled – easy doesn't mean boring!

AIM OF THE GAME:
To get rid of all your cards as fast as you can!

TO START

1. All the players pick a card from the deck. The person with the highest card becomes the dealer.

2. The dealer takes the cards and shuffles them as hard as he or she can. The dealer deals the cards out face down until all the players have seven cards each.

3. All the other cards are collected into a stack in the middle. To start the game, one card is taken from the top of the stack and put face up next to it. This is the widow.

HOW TO PLAY

1. Now all you have to do is cover up the widow with one of the seven cards in your hand. The card you play must be of the same rank or suit as the widow.

2. If you don't have a card that you can put down, you have to take a card from the stack and your pile will get bigger instead of smaller!

3. Then it is the next person's turn to do the same thing. It's better to put down higher cards if you have the choice.

4. Once all the cards from the stack are gone, everyone carries on playing from the cards in their hands, and if you can't put a card down, then you miss a turn.

WHO'S THE WINNER?

The person who runs out of cards first is the winner! To find out who comes second and third, turn all the cards over and add up the numbers on your cards. Picture cards count as ten points and an Ace counts as 15 points. The person with the most points is the loser and the person with the least points is second.

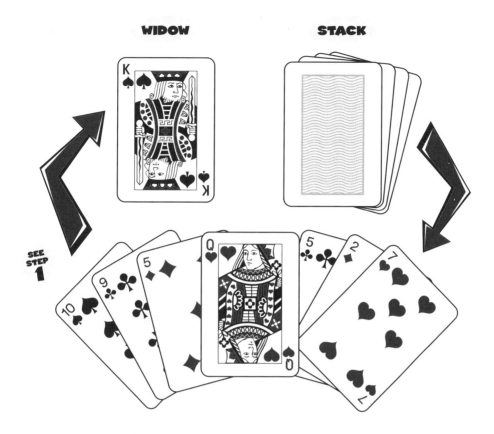

WIDOW   **STACK**

SEE STEP 1

WINNING WAY

Just in case you don't win (you never know, it might happen!), try to get rid of your higher-value cards as early as possible. To this end, when you cover the widow with a card of matching suit (rather than rank), you should try to put down an Ace, a court card or the highest-valued pip card you can. That way, if you don't get rid of all of your cards, your deficit total won't be too high and you'll have a chance of coming second.

TOO EASY?

Try giving certain cards **SPECIAL POWERS**. For instance, you could include the jokers and suggest that their special powers mean the next person has to pick up five cards unless they can cover the joker with another joker. If they do so, then the next person will have to pick up ten!

CHASE THE ACE

AGES: 5+

SKILL LEVEL: ▌

GOOD FOR: After-dinner entertainment.

One card, no complicated rules and little scope for ponderous tactical play make Chase the Ace the perfect party warm-up game.

AIM OF THE GAME:
To avoid being left with the lowest-ranked card.

TO START

1. Players are each given three individually wrapped sweets, which represent the three lives they have in Chase the Ace.

2. A standard 52-card deck is required. The deck is shuffled and each player takes a card, with the player drawing the lowest card appointed dealer for the game.

3. The dealer places one card face down in front of each player. At this stage the players do not look at their cards.

HOW TO PLAY

1. The game starts with the player to the left of the dealer. He or she picks up their card and looks at it. Their aim is to hold the highest card possible: Kings are high, Aces are low and the suits rank with spades the highest, then hearts, then diamonds and lastly clubs.

2. If the player holds a King, he or she must place it face up in front of them.

3. If they hold any other card, they can either stand (in other words stick with the card they hold), or exchange the card with the player to their left. The player cannot refuse and must hand over their card.

4. The turn passes around the table in a clockwise direction. When it reaches the dealer, he or she can elect to either stand or exchange their card with the top card from the remaining stack of cards.

5. When all players have had their turn, the cards are turned over. The player with the lowest card puts one of their three sweets into the centre of the table; they now have only two lives left.

6. The cards are gathered up, shuffled and dealt once again. The deal moves around the table clockwise and the game continues until all but one player has run out of sweets.

WHO'S THE WINNER?

The last player left with sweets is the winner. Their prize can either be the pool of sweets lost by their opponents or, if you would rather avoid the inevitable sugar rush that comes with such confectionary consumption, you can take back the sweets and award a more suitable prize.

WINNING WAY

The only way to improve your chances of winning at Chase the Ace is to make sure you make a sensible decision about whether to hold or exchange your original card. Play the percentages and bear in mind that you do not have to win the hand – you just have to avoid coming last. There are no prizes for the player with the highest-rank card, only penalties for the player left holding the lowest.

AUTHORS

AGES: 6+

SKILL LEVEL: ▮▮

GOOD FOR: Mixed gatherings and children's parties.

PLAYERS: 3–9

Lively, interactive and demanding, Authors is the perfect game with which to start the card playing at a children's party or family gathering.

AIM OF THE GAME:
To collect complete sets of cards of the same denomination.

TO START

1. Authors can be played with as many as nine players and as few as three. Get everybody seated around a table and ask each player to draw a card from a shuffled deck. The player who draws the highest-ranking card is appointed the dealer for the first hand; thereafter the job of dealer moves around the table in a clockwise fashion.

2. The dealer deals cards one at a time to each player, starting with the person seated to their left. The whole deck is used and distributed as evenly as possible. Some players will end up with more cards than others (unless, of course, you have four players), but this inequity will even itself out providing the deal rotates.

3. Players should keep their cards concealed from their opponents and should take some time to familiarize themselves with their hands, grouping the cards together by rank.

HOW TO PLAY

1. The player to the left of the dealer (let's call him Charlie) starts the game by asking any other player (in this case Linus) to give him a particular card, say, for example, the Ace of diamonds. If Linus has the Ace of diamonds, he must give it to Charlie.

2. Players can only ask for a card if they already hold another card of the same rank. So, back to our example, for Charlie to ask for the Ace of diamonds he must already hold an Ace from one of the other three suits.

3. If Charlie's bid is successful, his turn continues until he asks for a card from a player who doesn't hold the card he seeks. When this happens, the turn passes to the player asked.

4. When a player has collected all four cards of a particular rank, he or she must place the cards face down in front of them.

5. If a player runs out of cards, he or she can take no further part in the current deal. If their hand is emptied by the completion of a set of cards (rather than by another player successfully bidding for his or her final card), the turn passes to the player from whom they collected their last card.

WHO'S THE WINNER?

When all the cards have been played, the players count up the number of completed sets of cards they have collected. The player with the most is the winner of that hand and is given a bonus of ten points. Each player is also awarded a point for every set of cards gathered during the deal. Scores are recorded and the player with the highest aggregate total over a set number of deals is the winner. Alternatively, the game can be played in a 'first past the post' style, with the first to exceed 25 points crowned champion.

WINNING WAY

Authors is more a game of fun than strategy and should not be taken too seriously. However, for those competitive souls who must be first at everything, it is advantageous to make a mental note of the cards asked for by opponents.

PIG

AGES: 6+

SKILL LEVEL: ▌▌

GOOD FOR: Those looking for an alternative to 'pass the parcel' and other hackneyed party game 'classics'.

Whether played for prizes or fun, this is a game sure to delight children, who will relish the opportunity to play cards, act silly, point to their noses and call one another pigs!

AIM OF THE GAME:
To collect a hand made up of four-of-a-kind.

TO START

1. Seat the children around a table or in a circle on the floor. Clear the general area and stand back.

2. Take a standard 52-card deck and sort the cards by rank so that you end up with 13 complete sets. You will need one complete set per player, so, for example, if you have five players, you could use the court cards and Aces. It doesn't matter which rank of cards you choose as the object of the game is to be the first player to assemble four-of-a-kind with no preference given to the value of the cards. Put the remainder of the cards to one side and, presuming our example of five players, shuffle the 20 cards you have selected.

TWIST IN THE TAIL

To maintain the interest of players who are 'out' – and thereby avoid that awkward situation where only two are engaged in the game and the rest of the little pigs are making a sty out of your house – you can introduce a fun new rule. The redundant pigs are allowed to try to distract the active players by talking to them, but should any of them speak back to the ostracized swine, they are out too.

3. Each player is dealt four cards face down in front of them. When all the cards are dealt, the players pick up their hands and prepare to play.

HOW TO PLAY

1. The gameplay in Pig is continuous rather than alternate, so instead of one player leading off, the supervising adult calls 'Start'. The game commences with the players discarding a card to their left-hand neighbour and picking up the card that, by the same process, arrives at their right.

2. The game continues, with players discarding and receiving cards one by one, until one of the players completes a four-of-a-kind hand. When this feat is achieved, the triumphant player points to his or her nose without saying anything.

3. As soon as a player points to his or her nose, the others should do likewise. The last player to point to their nose loses the hand.

WHO'S THE WINNER?

When a player loses a hand, they are given a letter from the word 'pig' as a penalty. The object of the game is to avoid collecting three letters and spelling out the word. If you are playing Pig at a children's party, you may want to avoid confusion and argument by writing the letters on some sticky labels and handing them to the losing player at the end of each hand. The game continues until only one player is left. Prizes can be given to the victor in the usual fashion … with a chocolate pig an ideal reward.

DONKEY

AGES: 6+

SKILL LEVEL: ▐▐

GOOD FOR: When children get bored of playing Pig.

PLAYERS: 4–13

This game is a simplified version of Pig that is sure to delight fans of the original and newcomers alike.

AIM OF THE GAME:
To collect a complete set of four-of-a-kind.

TO START

1. The rules of Donkey are similar to those of Pig (see page 82). The cards are sorted by an adult prior to playing the game, and the same number of complete sets of four cards of the same denomination are used as there are players.

2. The sorted cards are shuffled and four are dealt to each player. The supervising adult then puts out the prizes for the game, with one piece of individually wrapped sweets laid out for all but one of the players (so, if there are six players in the game, there will be only five prizes).

HOW TO PLAY

1. The supervising adult calls 'Swap' and the game starts with the players discarding a card to their left-hand neighbour and picking up the card which, by the same process, arrives at their right.

2. When all players are ready, the adult calls 'Swap' again and the process is repeated.

3. The game continues, with players discarding and receiving cards one by one, until they complete a four-of-a-kind hand. When this feat is achieved, the player puts down his or her cards and takes a piece of confectionery.

WHO'S THE WINNER?

The winner of the game is the first player to complete a four-of-a-kind hand. However, there is no additional prize for coming first. Coming last, though, is something to be avoided, as there is no prize to the player who fails to complete a set.

This card moves
to the next player.

This card joins the hand,
completing four-of-a-kind

WINNING WAY

Donkey, like Pig, is for the most part a game of chance. Players should be
encouraged to keep their options open for as long as possible and should try to
remember the cards they have already passed on, but aside from that,
it's all down to luck!

NEWMARKET
OR BOODLE, STOPS

AGES: 7+

SKILL LEVEL: ▮▮

GOOD FOR: Rummy graduates.

A versatile game that can keep things moving at family parties but that can also occupy rowdy youngsters eager for prizes or those in search of a boredom cure on a rainy day.

AIM OF THE GAME:
To be the first player to get rid of all their cards ...
and along the way to collect more counters than your opponents!

TO START

1. Players each pick a card from the deck, and whoever chooses the lowest card becomes the dealer.

2. After shuffling and cutting the deck, the dealer distributes the cards as evenly as possible to the players. He or she also deals out a dummy hand, which they place to one side along with any spare cards.

3. Before the players look at their cards, the dealer takes four cards from a separate pack and lays them face up on the table. These are called the boodle cards and they must be an Ace, King, Queen and Jack each from different suits; so, for example, the Jack of spades, Queen of diamonds, King of hearts and Ace of clubs.

4. The players are each given ten counters, which they must place on the boodle cards (they are also given another ten counters, which they keep in reserve). They can place all ten counters on one card, but more often will spread them around.

HOW TO PLAY

1. With the stakes placed, the player to the left of the dealer leads off. He or she can play a card of any suit, but it must be the lowest card that they hold in that suit.

2. Play is continuous rather than alternate, and the next player to go is the one who holds the next-highest card in the suit. So, for example, if Player One had laid the seven of hearts, the player who holds the eight of hearts would go next.

DUMMY HAND

3. The play continues in this way until either the play is blocked because the card needed is tucked away in the dummy hand, or because the run is complete (Aces are high, so the appearance of an Ace automatically brings the run to an end).

4. Play is restarted by the person who played the last card, and resumes with them leading the lowest card of another suit. If, however, they do not hold any cards from another suit, the job of leading off passes to the player on their left.

5. When a player plays a card identical to one of the boodle cards, they receive all the counters that have been staked on that particular card.

WHO'S THE WINNER?

The player who gets rid of all their cards first wins the hand. The victor receives one counter from each player in respect of every card they still hold at the time they emptied their hand. If no player manages to get rid of all their cards, the winner is the player with fewest cards when the game becomes blocked. In these circumstances, the winner is entitled to one counter from each of their rivals in respect of the difference between the cards they have left and those they still hold in hand. So, for example, if David had three cards left at the end of the game and his rivals Stewart and Sharon each had five, they would both have to pay the victorious David two counters.

WINNING WAY

Consider carefully your options when leading off, as this is your opportunity to control the game. Watch the cards played and try to work out which cards your opponents hold. As the game develops, you may be able to frustrate your rivals by playing high-ranking cards that rid you of a particular suit without allowing them the opportunity to do likewise.

GAMES FOR PARTIES

RED DOG

OR HIGH CARD POOL

AGES: 7+

SKILL LEVEL: ▮▮

GOOD FOR: Getting any children's party buzzing.

PLAYERS: 2–10

Red Dog is a game of chance that is best played for prizes at children's parties ... quick, tense and dramatic, it offers a roller-coaster ride that is guaranteed to get your soiree swinging.

AIM OF THE GAME:
To trump the top card of the stock with a higher-ranked card of the same suit.

TO START

1. Give every child a bag of individually wrapped confectionery to use as stakes and seat all the players around a table.

2. With younger children it is probably best to appoint an adult to act as dealer (and as de facto arbitrator in the event of any disputes). Older children can draw cards from a shuffled deck to determine the dealer; lowest card gets the job.

3. Before the cards are dealt, the players each put an agreed number of sweet treats (units) into the centre of the table to establish a pool. It is probably best to start with two per player.

4. Five cards are now dealt to each player (although if the number of players exceeds eight, each will receive only four). The players pick up their cards and assess them. A good hand is one that includes high-ranking cards of all four suits, with the four Kings offering the perfect hand and guaranteed victory. The remaining cards are placed face down in front of the dealer in a stock pile.

5. Players must now place their stakes prior to the game commencing. The player to the left of the dealer starts the bidding and must stake at least one unit. The maximum bid by any one player must not exceed the total number of units held in the pool (so, in our example, if there were five players, no individual could stake more than ten pieces of confectionery).

HOW TO PLAY

1. The player to the left of the dealer goes first. The dealer turns over the top card of the stock and turns it face up on the table.

2. If the player can beat it (with a higher-ranked card of the same suit), he or she shows the other players their superior card and collects the sweets from the pool. The winning player keeps their remaining cards and the pool is restocked with another two units from each player.

3. If the active player cannot beat the card turned over by the dealer, they turn over their hand of cards and their stake is added to the pool.

4. The game continues until all players have had their turn. If you wish to continue playing, the cards must be gathered up and a fresh deal made.

WHO'S THE WINNER?

The player with the most sweets is the winner … though his or her dentist may also consider themselves somewhat fortuitous. Of course, if you prefer not to give your children sweets, you can play for counters that can be totalled up at the end of the game, with a non-confectionary prize awarded to the final victor.

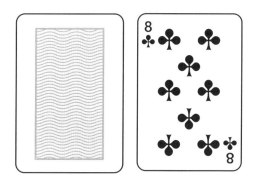

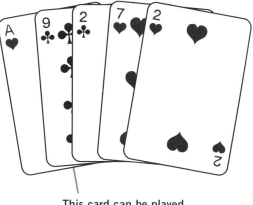

This card can be played to win the pool

WINNING WAY

If you have a great hand with lots of high-ranking cards, you will be tempted to stake big, but you may be wise to play more discreetly. A big stake may discourage your opponents from making a big bid themselves. A couple of overconfident, gung-ho players can soon boost the pool, so let them believe they are going to win and watch them throw their sweets away!

FE-FI-FO-FUM

AGES: 7+

SKILL LEVEL: ▌

GOOD FOR: The usual ranks of over-excited partygoers.

PLAYERS: 4–6

With a fairy-tale chant and prizes on offer, Fe-Fi-Fo-Fum is sure to make your party go with a swing.

AIM OF THE GAME:
To lay as many stop cards as possible and be the first player to empty your hand.

TO START

1. Deal out a well-shuffled pack between all the players. It doesn't matter if some players have an extra card; this inequity will even itself out if the starting point for the deal rotates with each hand.

HOW TO PLAY

1. The player to the left of the dealer leads off (or if a non-playing adult dealt the cards, start with the party host). He or she can play any card they wish, setting it down face up in the centre of the table. As they lay the card, they say 'Fe'.

2. The player who has the next card in ascending sequence and matching suit follows, playing the card and announcing it by saying 'Fi'. So, for example, if the game had opened with the four of hearts (Fe), the next card would be the five of hearts (Fi). The play continues with whoever holds the six, seven and eight, each player announcing their cards with calls of 'Fo', 'Fum' and 'Giant's tum' respectively.

3. The sequence ends when a player lays a card and calls 'Giant's tum'. The player who brought the run to a halt in this way starts the game off again by laying a new Fi card from his or her hand. Sequences do not go 'round the corner', so when a King is laid (irrespective of whether it is a Fe, Fi, Fo or Fum card), the sequence stops and is restarted by the player who played the King. Aces are low.

4. As the game develops, more and more cards will become stop cards because the next card in sequence has already been played. For example, following the opening sequence of the four to eight of hearts, the three of hearts would now become a stop card. When it is played, the run ends and the player who laid it starts a new sequence with a fresh Fe card.

WHO'S THE WINNER?

The first player to play all their cards is the winner. Continue playing until only one player is left holding cards. If you want to add a little spice to the proceedings, you can lay out individually wrapped sweets as prizes. Put out enough sweets for all but one of the players … he or she who comes last gets nothing.

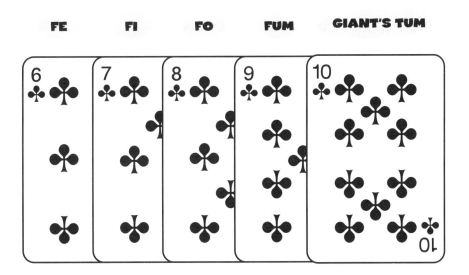

WINNING WAY

You can play this game strategically if you wish, plotting which card will give you the best opportunity to lay a stop card and thereby give you the chance to lay a Fe card. However, the feverish excitement of a children's party is no environment for ponderous tactical thinking. Keep the game moving quickly and play for fun.

KEMPS

AGES: 7+

SKILL LEVEL: ▮▮▮

GOOD FOR: Spicing up family gatherings with a little competitive card-based team play.

PLAYERS: 4–8

A little subterfuge and a whole lot of tension makes Kemps a children's party classic.

AIM OF THE GAME:
To collect four-of-a-kind and alert your partner to your success so that they can call a halt to the hand.

Four-of-a-kind.

TO START

1. Players are divided into pairs and each team takes a moment in private to discuss the signals they will use during the game. Once all is agreed, the players reconvene and the cards are cut to decide who will deal; the player with the lowest card becomes the dealer.

2. Four cards are dealt face down to each player, with an additional widow hand dealt face up to the centre of the table. The remainder of the cards are placed in a stack on the table.

HOW TO PLAY

1. The players pick up their cards and when the dealer says 'Go' they begin exchanging cards with the widow hand. They can only exchange one card at a time, but may do so continuously; there is no need to wait until an opponent has taken a turn. If two players go for the same card, the first of them to touch it gets it; younger children may need a little supervision (or first aid) in such circumstances.

2. When the players have taken all the cards they wish from the widow hand, the dealer takes away the four cards and deals out replacements from the stack of unused cards. When the new cards are laid out, the dealer says 'Go' again and the card swapping resumes.

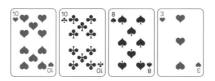

PLAYER 3

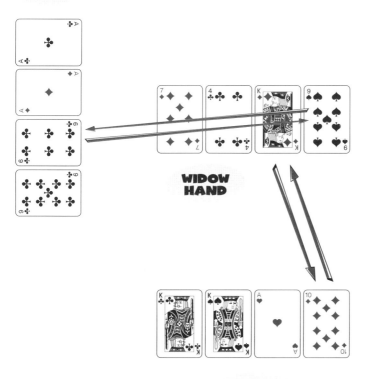

PLAYER 2

PLAYER 4

WIDOW HAND

PLAYER 1

3. The hand carries on in this fashion until one of the players calls it to a halt or the stock of cards runs out. If the latter situation occurs and the hand reaches a stalemate, it is ruled a draw and has no impact on the outcome of the game. However, a positive outcome for the game can be achieved in two ways:

A CALL OF 'KEMPS'

If a player achieves a hand made up of four-of-a-kind, he or she must try to alert their team-mate to the fact. They cannot themselves call the hand to a halt, but must instead rely upon the system of signals agreed between the two prior to the game. Signals cannot be verbal and are usually gestures or body movements. Players are also not allowed to deliberately try to confuse opponents by using signals when they do not have four-of-a-kind. When a player detects that his or her team-mate has completed a set, they should immediately call 'Kemps'. The hand is brought to an end and the player in question reveals his or her cards. If the call is correct, that team wins the hand; however, if the partner misinterpreted the signal and called the game prematurely, the hand goes to the opposing team.

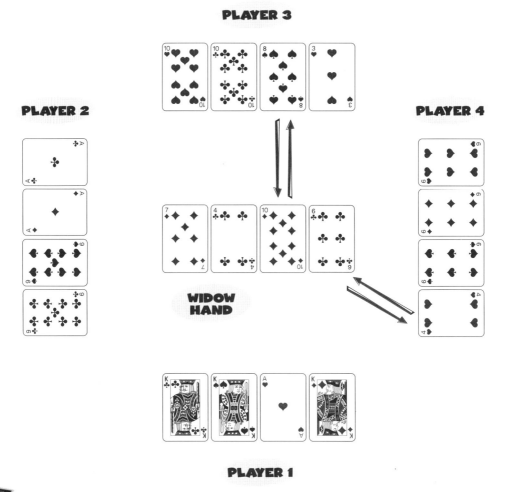

PLAYER 3

PLAYER 2

PLAYER 4

WIDOW HAND

PLAYER 1

A CALL OF 'STOP KEMPS'

A hand can also be won by a player who intercepts a signal and calls 'Stop Kemps' before his or her rival has a chance to halt the hand. So, for example, if you see an opponent raise an eyebrow in very deliberate fashion while looking directly at his or her team-mate, you may want to take the risk of calling 'Stop Kemps' on the grounds that they are probably signalling that they have completed a winning hand. If you call it correctly, your team will win the hand, but if when the cards are checked the opposing team has not yet assembled four-of-a-kind, you lose.

WHO'S THE WINNER?

Each time a team loses a hand, it is given a letter from the word 'kemps' as punishment. The object of the game is to avoid collecting five letters and spelling out the word. The first team to lose five hands is, in effect, the loser of the game. If you are playing with more than two teams, keep going until only one is left.

WINNING WAY

Signals must be clear, simple and should be used at an agreed time during each hand. For example, rubbing the tip of your right index finger when the dealer collects up the cards and re-deals the widow hand. A lingering gesture of this kind is far more likely to be picked up than something more fleeting that might be missed. You should also try to observe the cards other players are going for: if your playing partner picks up a card and you have a matching one, you should think about discarding it. You should also watch what your opponents are picking up and when possible block them by hanging onto sought-after cards.

CHEAT

Although it is against the rules to use fake signals to induce other players to call 'Stop Kemps', if you're clever about it, you can definitely get your rivals twitching with a few carefully employed moves. Surely they can't think that you'd sniff and scratch your nose solely to mislead them ... perish the thought!

GAMES
FOR
PRIZES

31s

If you can add up to 31 you're old enough to play this game, and what's more you'll love it ... but only when you win.

AIM OF THE GAME:
To hold a hand of 31 ... the clue's in the name.

TO START

1. A full deck of cards is used and all players should be given an equal amount of individually wrapped sweets to use as stakes.

2. Before the deal is made, players agree a stake for the hand which is placed into a central kitty.

3. The cards are cut to determine the dealer, and the deal passes around the table clockwise with each hand.

4. All players are dealt three cards, which are placed face down in front of them. Three additional cards are laid face up in a row in the centre of the table (this is called the widow hand).

HOW TO PLAY

1. In traditional fashion, the player to the left of the dealer goes first. He or she must swap one card from their hand for one of the cards in the widow hand. They cannot pass and cannot exchange more than one card at a time.

2. The turn passes around the table clockwise, with players swapping cards one by one.

WHO'S THE WINNER?

1. The game comes to a halt either when one player has a hand of 31 (Aces count 11) or when any player 'knocks' because they are confident that their hand – though imperfect – is better than their opponents'.

2. The situation when a player has 31 should be clear enough – they automatically win and collect the kitty.

3. The scenario where a player knocks is less obvious. A player can knock at any time during the game and at that point all cards are turned face up. The hands are checked and the winner is the player with the best hand.

4. A hand of 31 is the grail; thereafter, a hand that contains three cards of equal rank is next in value; failing that, the winner is the player who has the highest total in any one suit.

5. However, when a player chooses to 'knock', his or her opponents get one more turn at exchanging their cards with the widow hand before turning over their cards.

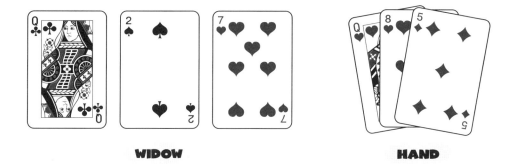

WIDOW **HAND**

WINNING WAY

Hang onto any pairs of cards in the early part of the game; if you get the chance to complete a trio while your opponents are still pondering their options, you are likely to catch them off guard. Going for a perfect hand of 31 is unwise unless you hold an Ace; you cannot achieve such a hand without capturing one of these four elusive cards. By contrast, snaring two of the 12 court cards to complete the hand should be easier, as you only need two cards from 12. As always, play the percentages and give yourself the best chance of winning those sweets.

BLIND HOOKEY

AGES: 7+

SKILL LEVEL: ▮▮

GOOD FOR: Children's parties and large family gatherings.

PLAYERS: 3–10

It may be a game of chance, but children will take Blind Hookey very seriously. Losing is not easily accepted, but winning is often greeted with greater glee than you might expect.

AIM OF THE GAME:
To reveal a card of higher value than the banker.

TO START

1. Players are seated around a table and a full pack of 52 cards is needed. You will also need a stock of counters (of the kind used for board games) to use as stakes.

2. The cards are cut to determine the banker for the hand; the player with the lowest card deals. There is no dealer in Blind Hookey.

3. The shuffled deck is passed to the player on the left of the banker, who removes a small stack of cards (probably around five or six) and places them face down on the table in front of him or her. The remainder of the deck is passed to the player on their left, who does the same.

4. The deck of cards moves around the table in a clockwise direction until it reaches the banker, who also removes a small stack of cards in the same way as the other players. The remainder of the deck is set aside and won't be needed until the next deal.

GAMES FOR PRIZES

HOW TO PLAY

1. The players now place their stakes. An upper limit should be set, with perhaps five counters the maximum per deal. Counters are placed above the relevant stack of face-down cards according to the player's confidence of revealing a card that is higher in value than the banker's. Aces are low.

2. When all stakes are laid, the banker turns over his or her stack of cards to expose the bottom card. The others now turn over their cards one by one, starting with the player to the left of the banker.

3. The banker wins from all players whose exposed cards are lower than or equal to his or hers, but pays to anybody who shows a card of higher value.

WHO'S THE WINNER?

Continue to play successive hands until everybody has had a turn as banker. Any players who run out of counters drop out of the game. The winner is the player with the most counters at the end of play. If you are playing at a children's party, you may want to exchange the victor's pile of counters for a small prize … perhaps a book on children's card games?

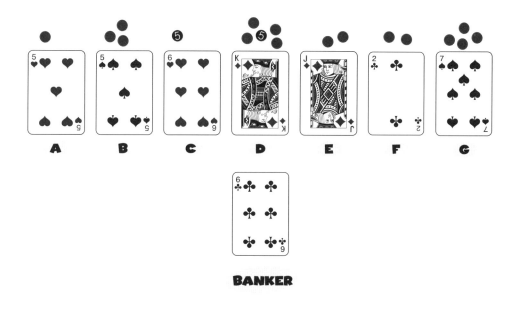

A   B   C   D   E   F   G

BANKER

WINNING WAY

Without recommending you cheat by looking at your cards – which would obviously be wrong – there is little you can do to improve your chances of winning a hand of Blind Hookey. All we can recommend is that you stake wisely throughout the game and don't throw your counters away early in the game. Let your opponents be the ones to play boldly and badly.

TWENTY-ONE
OR VINGT-ET-UN, PONTOON, BLACK JACK

AGES: 7+ (younger players will enjoy playing a simplified game without stakes)

SKILL LEVEL: ■■■

GOOD FOR: Break-time card players and other competitive souls.

PLAYERS: 2–10

With no complicated set-ups and no impenetrable rules, Twenty-one is the undoubted king of prize-winning card games.

AIM OF THE GAME:
To hold a hand with a value of 21,
or as near as possible.

BACKGROUND

Twenty-one is, in principle, a simple game. Each player starts with two cards and can take additional cards from the deck one by one, as they try to complete a hand of 21 without exceeding this figure. The traditional banking version of Pontoon takes this simple game and adds a legion of complicated rules, which can often take the fun out of the game for kids. By way of compromise, I have outlined a variant of the game that combines elements of the senior game with the simplistic game frequently played by children without stakes.

TO START

1. An adult or reliable child is given the job of banker/dealer. In our game, the banker does not play but merely deals the cards and distributes the winnings. He or she starts the job by giving each player a set number of counters (25 is a good number to start with). The remainder goes to the bank.

2. The banker gives each player one card, which is dealt face down onto the table. Players look at their cards and place their stakes. A maximum and minimum starting stake should be set (I would recommend a minimum of one counter and a maximum of three counters).

HOW TO PLAY

1. Once all players have placed their stakes, the dealer hands round a second card to each player.

2. The players look at their cards and assess their options; they each now have a chance to improve their hand if they are bold enough! The player to the left of the banker goes first, with the turn moving around the table clockwise thereafter. Players can either:

'BUY': This is where they take an additional card and add to their stake. The additional stake must not exceed the maximum, but can be no less than the original amount they staked at the start of the game. Players can immediately buy a fourth and fifth card if they want, but on each occasion they must add to their stake again. Alternatively, they can stop buying cards and twist (see above right). For example, a player who has a ten and two may elect to buy a card first, but if the card dealt is another two, they may decide to be cautious and twist for their fourth card.

'TWIST': If a player decides to twist, he or she does not add to their stake but simply takes another card from the dealer. Once a player has started twisting, they cannot subsequently 'buy', so their stake remains the same.

'STICK': If a player is happy with his or her two cards, either because they add up to 21 or because they are close to that total, they may decide to stick with them. He or she puts them on the table face down and takes no further cards. In our game we will make it a rule that players cannot stick with a total of 15 or under.

3. Players continue to twist and buy cards until either their total exceeds 21, at which point they are said to have 'bust', or they decide to stick.

4. When all players have finished their bidding, the banker asks them to turn over their cards.

WILD CARDS

In some games, the rules allow 'wild cards' which can represent cards of any value. This is particularly useful in games where runs or sequences are built up. The cards most commonly used as wild cards are the Jokers, the twos (also known as deuces, giving the call 'Deuces wild') and the Jacks, although other cards can be used if wanted. If only two wild cards are wanted, it's usual to use the black Jacks rather than the red ones.

WHO'S THE WINNER?

The winning hand is that which totals closest to 21. A hand comprised of an Ace and a ten is called 'pontoon', but an Ace and a court card supersedes this and is called 'royal pontoon'. If no player holds such a hand, then any combination that adds up to 21 is victorious. Failing that, the total closest to 21 wins. In the event of two players holding a hand of equal value, the bank pays both. All losing players are obliged to pay their stakes to the banker, while the victors receive payment equal to their stakes from the banker.

A winning hand, totalling 21.

A 'royal pontoon'.

CARD VALUES

In pontoon, the Aces are high or low (that is, they count as one or 11) and the court cards (King, Queen and Jack) count as 10.

SWEET SIXTEEN

AGES: 7+

SKILL LEVEL: ▮▮▮

GOOD FOR: Youngsters who are bored of Pontoon but eager for a competitive game of cards.

PLAYERS: 2–10

Two cards, a banker and a simple target – this game is as sweet as its name.

AIM OF THE GAME:
To hold two cards with a combined value of 16.

TO START

1. Before the game can start, the players must agree upon stakes and upon the number of deals over which the game will be played. It's probably best to play for five deals and to award points according to the scoring guide outlined opposite. Counters can be used to aid scoring. Each player should start with ten counters, but don't forget that the bank will need to be well stocked too!

2. Next, a banker must be appointed, with the players each cutting the deck; whoever gets the lowest card gets the job. The banker removes the eights and sixes (with the exception of the eight of diamonds) from the deck. The remaining 45 cards are shuffled and passed to the player seated to the left of the banker, in this case that man is Sam.

HOW TO PLAY

1. Sam takes the top two cards from the deck, which is positioned face down in front of him. His aim is to hold two cards with a value of 16 (Aces are low and court cards each count ten).

2. He can swap his cards one at a time, discarding one of the cards held onto a waste pile and taking the top card from the deck. Sam can continue changing cards to get closer to the grail of 16. However, if he exceeds 16, his hand will 'bust' and his turn comes to an end. He may choose to avoid this situation by electing to stick on any total under 16.

3. A player does not tell his or her opponents what he or she has scored – even if they have bust – but instead simply puts their cards face-down in front of them. They now shuffle the deck, mixing in the cards from the waste pile, and pass it to the player seated to their left.

WHO'S THE WINNER?

1. The game continues until all players have had their turn. The cards are then revealed, with each player turning their hand over simultaneously on the word of the banker. Counters can then be awarded on the following basis:

• Players with 16 exactly receive as many counters from the bank as there are players in the game.

• Players with 16 exactly in a hand that includes the eight of diamonds receive two counters from the bank for each player in the game.

• Players with less than 16 pay the banker one counter.

• Players with more than 16 pay the banker one counter for every pip above 16.

• Ten bonus counters are awarded to the player with the best hand. In the event of a tie, the counters are shared.

2. At the end of ten deals, the counters are totted up. The player with the most wins the prize … which could be a week without having to do the dishes or some sweets if you're feeling generous.

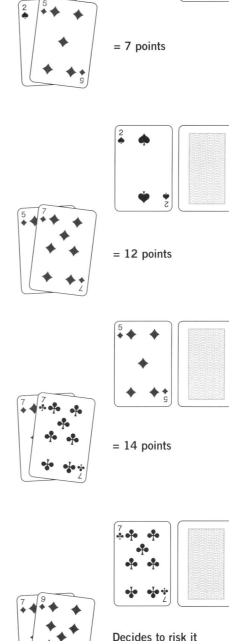

= 7 points

= 12 points

= 14 points

Decides to risk it
= 16 points
Stick!

RACING

AGES: 7+

SKILL LEVEL: ▮

GOOD FOR: Noisy children's parties and rowdy get-togethers.

PLAYERS: Any number

Whatever it lacks in strategy and equine presence, this card game makes up for in pure excitement. Never has such drama been unleashed with just 52 cards, some counters and a few confectionary-based prizes.

AIM OF THE GAME:
To predict which suit's Ace will be first to reach the finish line.

TO START

1. Before the game starts, you'll need to gather up some counters. Give each player ten counters and make it clear that the game will be played over five races (deals).

2. Appoint a reliable child or an adult as dealer/banker and pass them a standard 52-card deck.

3. The dealer removes the Aces from the deck and places them in a row at the top of the table. He or she then places the top seven cards from the deck in a vertical column below the Aces. The layout should look like a T when complete.

HOW TO PLAY

1. The players now place their stakes, putting their counters next to the Ace they think will win the race. They can bid as many counters as they want; if they choose the winning Ace correctly, the banker will give them back their stake plus an identical number of counters. Of course, if they lose, their counters go to the bank.

2. When all stakes have been laid, the remaining 41 cards are shuffled and turned face down in a stack on the table. The dealer now turns the cards over one by one. The rank of the card revealed is unimportant but the suit is not; each time a particular suit appears, the corresponding Ace moves forward one place in the layout. So, for example, if the dealer turns over the five of clubs, the Ace of clubs will move forward one place.

3. The winning post is the seventh card in the layout, so the first Ace to pass that point is victorious. At the end of each hand, the banker distributes the winnings (in counters) to the players who successfully guessed which Ace would win.

WHO'S THE WINNER?

The person with the most counters at the end of five hands is the winner.
A set prize, perhaps a chocolate bar, is awarded to the triumphant player.

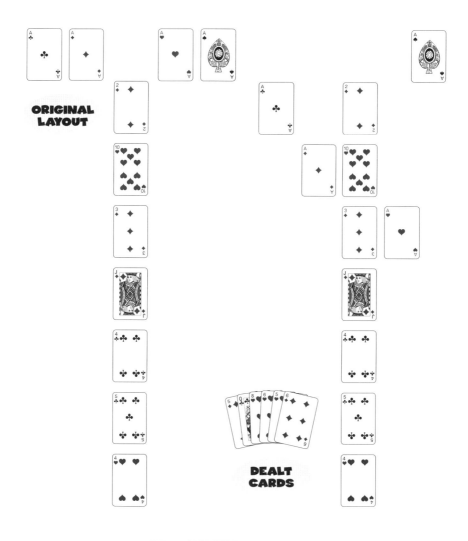

ORIGINAL LAYOUT

DEALT CARDS

WINNING WAY

The seven cards laid out vertically in the layout (the stem of the T) offer the only
hint of what might happen when the race begins. If there are three or four cards of
a particular suit in the layout, the chances of the corresponding Ace winning the
race are greatly reduced. Aside from that, Racing is purely a game of chance.

LIFT SMOKE

AGES: 7+

SKILL LEVEL: ▋▋▋

GOOD FOR: Introducing children to card games that use 'tricks'.

PLAYERS: 4–6

An engaging but straightforward trick-based game that is sure to stir the interest of budding card players and veterans alike.

AIM OF THE GAME:

To win more tricks than your opponents and thereby be the last player left with cards held in hand.

TO START

1. A shuffled deck is placed face down in the centre of the table and each player turns over the top card in turn. The player revealing the lowest-ranked card (Aces are high) is appointed dealer.

2. The player to the left of the dealer cuts the deck to establish the trump suit. The cards are then shuffled once more and dealt.

3. Each player is given the same number of cards (one by one) as there are players taking part in the game. The remainder of the cards are placed in the centre of the table to form a stock.

4. The players now take up their cards and hold them in hand, away from the view of their opponents, and the trick playing begins.

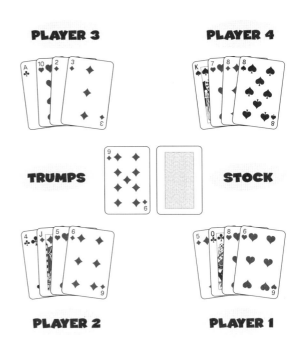

PLAYER 3

PLAYER 4

TRUMPS

STOCK

PLAYER 2

PLAYER 1

PLAYER 3

PLAYER 4

Player Three's Ace might have won the trick, but Player Four had no clubs and had to trump.

PLAYER 2

PLAYER 1

HOW TO PLAY

1. The player to the left of the dealer starts the game, playing one of his or her cards onto the table to lead the trick.

2. The turn now moves around the table in a clockwise direction. The second player must try to build on the trick but must follow in suit, or if they cannot play a card of the same suit, they can trump. If they can do neither, they discard a card onto the trick, thereby reducing their hand.

3. The dealer plays last and when he or she has had their turn the trick is complete.

4. The trick is won by the highest-rank trump played or if no trumps have been played, the highest card in the suit led.

5. The dealer gathers up the completed trick, places it to one side and gives the trick winner the top card from the stock. The winner, who now has more cards than his or her opponents, leads the next trick.

WINNING WAY

As with any trick-based game, the key to success is to make a mental note of the cards played and of the suits your opponents are unable to follow.

PRIZE-WINNING

You may like to add to the interest by rewarding each trick winner with a small confectionary prize. Additional prizes can be awarded to the overall game winner.

WHO'S THE WINNER?

When a player runs out of cards, he or she drops out of the game. Play continues until either only one player is left holding cards or the stock of cards runs dry. In the event of the latter situation, the winner of the next trick is deemed the game winner.

MONTE BANK

AGES: 8+

SKILL LEVEL: ▮▮▮

GOOD FOR: Those who enjoy the role of being banker.

PLAYERS: 4–6

Monte Bank is a simple game of chance that can be played at parties or for fun, but that must always be played for stakes.

AIM OF THE GAME:
To predict which section of the layout includes a card of the same suit to that revealed by the banker.

TO START

1. Players each cut a shuffled deck to determine who will be banker; the player revealing the highest-ranked card becomes the banker.

2. Each player is given ten counters or similar items to use as stakes. The counters should be of different colours or in some way discernible from those of their opponents … we don't want the banker getting mixed up and paying out to the wrong player!

3. The banker removes the eights, nines and tens from the pack of cards, shuffles them once more and deals out four cards face up in a grid. The top two cards are called the 'top layout' and the bottom pair are the 'bottom layout'.

GAMES FOR PRIZES

HOW TO PLAY

1. The players now place their stakes. You can have as many players as you wish, but you should set minimum and maximum stake limits (one and five counters respectively is a good starting point). Counters are staked on either the top or bottom layout.

WHO'S THE WINNER?

When all stakes are laid, the dealer takes the top card from the remainder of the deck. This card is called 'the gate', and if it is of a matching suit to any of the four face-up cards, the banker must pay out to those players who placed their stakes next to that half of the layout. See the example illustrated above right.

1. If the gate is of a different suit to all four cards in the layout, the banker collects all the counters.

2. After five deals, the job of banker rotates around the table, with the player to the left of the current incumbent taking over.

BOTTOM LAYOUT

STAKES

TOP LAYOUT

THE GATE

WINNING WAY

Monte Bank is entirely a game of chance. If it's your day, you'll clean up; if not, you'll win nothing. Whichever way, don't take it personally.

BRAG

AGES: 11+

SKILL LEVEL: ▮▮▮

GOOD FOR: Aspiring Poker players who want to play a more 'serious' game of cards.

PLAYERS: Up to 10

Simpler than Poker, but with all the drama of placing stakes and bluffing plus the opportunity to say 'I'll see you', Brag is a teenage card sharp's dream game.

AIM OF THE GAME:
To hold – or convince your opponents that you hold – a superior hand to your opponents.

TO START

1. Each player is given a pile of counters or individually wrapped sweets to use as stakes. The players then agree minimum and maximum stakes (one to five counters per bid is suggested).

2. After the cards have been cut and the lowest player has been appointed dealer, he or she places a minimum stake into the pot (the centre of the table). They then deal out three cards to each player, placing them face down one at a time onto the table.

3. The players collect their cards and assess their hands. The stake laying now begins.

HOW TO PLAY

1. The player to the left of the dealer starts the bidding. He or she stakes as much or as little as they want (provided they stay within the prescribed minimum and maximum levels). A high bet suggests they are confident that the hand they hold will be a winning one … although, of course, it might be a bluff.

2. The turn moves around the table in a clockwise direction, and each player can either match the bet, raise or fold. If a player folds, they do not have to stake any more counters and simply return their cards to the dealer. They will take no further part in the hand.

3. The betting continues, moving round and round the table for as long as it takes until all players still in the game bet the same amount and no player wishes to raise the stakes further. Of course, if one player out-stakes all the others and none of his or her opponents are prepared to match them, they win the hand automatically. In this situation they do not have to show their cards to the rest of the players – they will never know if the player was bluffing or had genuine cause for confidence.

WHO'S THE WINNER?

With the bidding over, the cards are turned over and the hands assessed. Three cards are wild and can be used to represent any other card to make a winning combination; these three cards – the Ace of diamonds, the Jack of clubs and the nine of diamonds – are called the braggers. Combinations of cards rank in the following order (with the best first):

Three natural Aces.

TRIOS (three of a kind will always beat a pair, irrespective of rank)
THREE NATURAL ACES (including the three of diamonds but no other braggers)
THREE ACES (including any two Aces and one of the other braggers)
THREE NATURAL KINGS
THREE KINGS (two Kings plus any of the braggers)

The pattern continues down to the three twos.

Natural pair.

PAIRS

The ranking of pairs is in keeping with the above, so a natural pair will always beat a pair of the same rank that consists of one natural card and a bragger.

SINGLETONS

If there are no pairs, the hand is won by the player who has the highest-ranked single card. Suits have no bearing on the outcome, so if two players have cards of the same rank, the pot is shared.

The player with the best hand – as you might expect – takes the kitty.

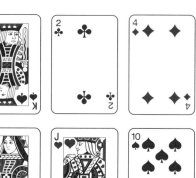

Although the second hand has more high cards in Brag, the King singleton beats them.

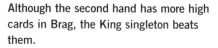

THREE-STAKE BRAG

AGES: 11+

SKILL LEVEL:

GOOD FOR: Teenage parties and other adolescent gatherings.

With three times the opportunity for stake laying, this is a Brag variant that is sure to delight those with a penchant for bluff and bravado.

AIM OF THE GAME:

To convince your opponents that you hold superior cards to them.

TO START

The preliminaries of Three-stake Brag are the same as for the single-stake variant (see page 114). However, in this game, stakes are placed after each card is dealt.

HOW TO PLAY

1. After the dealer has dealt one card to each player, the play is temporarily halted while stakes are placed. The players look at their card and bid as before. The players continue staking until they wish to go no further. The cards are revealed and the player with the highest-ranked card takes the pot. If two players have cards of equal status, the winnings are shared. There are no braggers (wild cards) in this first round.

2. The players leave their first card face up on the table and the dealer now hands them a second card. Another round of stake laying takes place, and when it reaches its conclusion cards are revealed. Braggers are now effective, so, for example, the Jack of clubs and the Queen of hearts count as a pair of Queens. The player with the highest-ranked pair wins the hand (natural pairs always beat an equally ranked pair that includes a bragger). If there are no pairs, the same rules apply as for the first round.

3. The two played cards are now left on the table and the dealer passes out a third card to each player. The now-familiar stake laying follows before the cards are revealed. This time, however, the rules about the best hand change, and the player whose cards total closest to 31 (either above or below) takes the kitty. Aces count as 11 and court cards are worth ten; all other cards have a value commensurate with their pips. Braggers are of no additional significance.

In Three-stake Brag, this hand is impossible to beat.

10 PTS **10 PTS** **11 PTS**

WINNING WAY

As in all versions of Brag, the ability to bluff rather than tactical genius is the greatest gift a player can have. You could spend hours trying to assess probabilities, but you are better off working on your powers of deceit and subterfuge!

GIN RUMMY
(FOR KIDS)

AGES: 11+

SKILL LEVEL: ▌▌▌

GOOD FOR: Rummy graduates and those eager to take their card playing to a new level.

This classic and enduringly popular game is a stepping stone for young card players eager for a fresh challenge.

AIM OF THE GAME:

To meld your hand into sets of cards that either run sequentially (for example, Jack, Queen, King of hearts) or that are equal in value (for example, three Aces). The more cards that you manage to collate into sets, the more chance you have of winning.

TO START

1. Each player is dealt ten cards, with the remainder of the deck placed face down in a neat stack in the centre of the table.

2. The top card of the central stack is turned over and placed face up alongside the stack.

HOW TO PLAY

1. The basic principle of the game is the same as Rummy (see page 62), so at each turn the active player can either take the top card from the face-down stack or the face-up card from the adjacent pile. He or she then discards one card.

2. The non-dealer starts the game. The objective is to meld your hand into sets of either three or four cards that run in sequence or are of equal value. If the face-up card helps achieve this goal, the player will take it; if not, he or she should pick up the unknown top card and try their luck.

3. The game continues, with players taking alternate turns until either one player declares that he or she is ready to 'go down' (see opposite) or the cards run out. If the latter occurs and the stack of face-down cards is spent, then the hand is ruled a draw and no points are awarded.

WHO'S THE WINNER?
(THE HAND)

When a player 'goes down', the hand is scored and – as you would expect – is won by the player with the best points score. Sounds simple enough, but what does it all mean?

GOING DOWN – Either player can elect to 'go down' (that is to say, they can bring the hand to a halt) providing they have no more than ten points against them in unmatched cards. The unmatched cards are any that do not form part of completed sets (that is, collections of three or four cards that run in sequence or that are equal in value). Unmatched cards count against you according to their face value, with court cards counting ten and Aces one. So, for example, if Phil has three Kings, the two, three, four and five of spades and three unmatched cards consisting of the four of hearts, the two of clubs and the three of diamonds, he can 'go down' with nine points against him. All he need say is 'Going down for nine'; he then turns his cards face up so that his opponent, Grant, sees his hand.

LAYING OFF – When a player decides to 'go down', he or she gives their opponent the privilege of laying off his or her unmatched cards to reduce their points deficit. Unmatched cards can be played onto the matched sequences put down by an opponent providing they either match in value or continue a sequence. So, in the example given above, Grant, who's hand consists of three Queens, three nines and four unmatched cards (the Ace of spades, the King of hearts, the two of diamonds and the Jack of hearts), now has the chance to get rid of some of his costly spare cards. He can play the King of hearts onto Phil's trio of Kings, and he can lose the Ace of spades by adding it to his opponent's sequence of spades. After laying off, Grant is now left with a minus score of 12 (the sum value of his two outstanding cards, the two of diamonds and the Jack of hearts).

CALLING GIN – A hand consisting of three completed sets of cards (that is to say, with no unmatched cards) is called 'Gin'. If a player goes down with a Gin hand, his or her opponent is not allowed to lay off any cards against him or her.

UNDERCUTTING – If a player chooses to 'go down' but loses the hand, his or her opponent is said to have undercut them. So, back to Phil and Grant, if Phil had gone down for nine only to find that Grant's score, once he had laid off any available cards, was seven, he would have lost the hand by two points.

PHIL

GRANT

−9

−12

WORDS TO REMEMBER

BOODLE CARDS: an Ace, King, Queen and Jack (each of different suits) that are taken from a separate pack and placed in a layout to be used in prize-winning games like Newmarket.

BRAGGERS: the Ace of diamonds, Jack of clubs and nine of diamonds which, in Bridge, are used as wild cards.

BUY: to increase the betting in a game of Twenty-one in order to draw a face-down card.

COURT CARDS: Jacks, Queens and Kings (also known as face cards).

DISCARD: to play a card that is neither a trump nor one that follows in suit.

FOLLOW SUIT: to play a card of the same suit as the card that led the trick or hand.

FOUNDATION CARDS: the cards upon which players build layouts in patience-style games.

GIN: a hand in Gin Rummy in which all the cards are melded together.

GO DOWN: choosing to end a game (usually of Rummy) early because you believe you have a winning hand.

JOKER: the name given to the two extra cards that come with a standard 52-card deck and that are used as trump cards in some games.

MELD: a matched set of three or more cards which run either in sequence or are identical in rank.

PAIR ROYAL: three cards of equal rank in Brag.

ROUND THE CORNER: the practice of allowing runs of cards to move from high to low in consecutive sequences, so for example, a King is followed by an Ace and then a two. A game that does not allow sequences to go 'round the corner' will see all runs stop when a King is played.

SINGLETON: an unmatched single card.

STOCK: the undealt part of a deck of cards which is usually placed face-down on the table during most games.

TALON: a stack of cards set aside for later use in a deal.

TWIST: request to be dealt an additional card in Twenty-one.

WHICH GAME?

AGE 7+

AGE 8+

AGE 9+

AGE 10+

AGE 11+

AGE 12+

SKILL LEVEL 1

SKILL LEVEL 2

WHICH GAME?

Observation; concentration; memory	Donkey	84–5
Observation; concentration; strategic thinking	Newmarket (Boodle, Stops)	86–7
Concentration; tactical thinking; judgement	Red Dog (High-card Pool)	88–9
Patience; judgement	**Games for Prizes:**	
	Blind Hookey	100–1

SKILL LEVEL 3

	Games for One:	
Patience; perseverance; logical thinking	Ace's Up	
	(Idiot's Delight)	15
Observation; concentration; patience	Stop The Clock (The Clock,	
	Clock Patience)	16–17
Observation; concentration; logical thinking	Golf (+ two-player option)	18–19
Observation; organization; patience; strategic thinking	Puss in the Corner	20–1
Patience; observation; concentration; logical thinking	Storehouse (Reserve)	29
	Games for Two:	
Concentration; quick thinking; rapid reactions	Spit (Speed)	44–5
Concentration; memory; tactical thinking	Colonel	46–7
	Games for Two or More:	
Concentration; strategic thinking; perseverance	Rummy	62–3
Concentration; strategic thinking; patience	Dry Jack	68–9
	Games for Parties:	
Recognition and differentiation; concentration	Go Boom!	
	(Rockaway)	76–7
Observation; memory; team-work; tactical thinking; rapid reactions	Kemps	92–3
	Games for Prizes:	
Observation; mental arithmetic; strategic thinking	31s	98–9
Observation; mental arithmetic; judgement	Twenty-one (Vingt-et-un, Pontoon, Black Jack)	102–5

SKILL LEVEL 4

SKILL LEVEL 5

INDEX

Executive Editor **Trevor Davies**
Project Editor **Kate Tuckett**
Design Manager **Tokiko Morishima**
Design & illustration **'ome design**
Senior Production Controller **Ian Paton**